LIKE MODERN EDENS

*Winegrowing in Santa Clara Valley
and Santa Cruz Mountains 1798-1981*
by Charles L. Sullivan
Foreword by Leon D. Adams

CALIFORNIA HISTORY CENTER
1982

Local History Studies ∘ Volume 28

Made possible by the membership of
the California History Center Foundation

Edited by John G. McArthur and Seonaid McArthur. Cover design by
Helen K. Davie. Index by Ruth Duckwald.

For Clyde Arbuckle and Robert Couchman

*The whole valley of San Jose seems
one great garden . . . In and around
the city are beautiful gardens and vineyards,*
like modern Edens.

— *J.Q.A. Warren (1863)*

TABLE OF CONTENTS

Grape harvest on the 70 acre C.A. Baldwin Vineyard, the present site of De Anza College, Cupertino.

A. Zicovich Cupertino Winery was cultivating 40 acres in 1895.

FOREWORD

Charles Sullivan's *Like Modern Edens* is an important contribution to the vinicultural history of Santa Clara, Santa Cruz, and San Mateo Counties. It amplifies with fascinating, hitherto unpublished details, the research during the 1940s by historians Irving McKee and Vincent Carosso, who traced the beginnings of Northern California winegrowing from the founding of Mission Santa Clara in 1777, whence it spread almost a half century later to regions north of San Francisco Bay.

Mr. Sullivan's book does much more. In its pages you meet scores of the pioneer vineyardists, for many of whom South Bay landmarks and streets are named. You read of how they nurtured their vines to early prize-winning greatness, only to see them die in the phylloxera epidemic, when many vineyards were replaced by prune orchards. You learn how fanatical Drys induced Californians to support state and national Prohibition laws; then about the scandals of the Prohibition era, and next of the post-Repeal years when urbanization paved over most of the remaining vineyards. Finally, Mr. Sullivan describes the present revival of fine vineyards in the Santa Cruz Mountains district in response to the wine revolution that has begun to civilize drinking in the United States.

His book is fascinating reading and a significant addition to the winegrowing history of California.

Leon D. Adams

PREFACE

Intelligent people interested in matters of the mind or the senses eventually find themselves seeking after the origins of this interest. They naturally become impatient when these origins are mysterious or obscured. Wine and winemaking are subjects about which Americans have become increasingly interested during the last two decades.

No state produces more wine than California and certainly there is no state more preoccupied with its own history. Yet the history of California winemaking is not only tantalizingly mysterious but has been obscured by the peculiar nature of the product—wine.

History sells wine, for age means quality to the average wine drinker. Ageing is what one does to wine to make it better. Tradition and longevity seem to imply quality, in a wine and for the winery that produced it. It follows that much which has passed as California wine history has been written with an eye on its commercial effect.

When a proper history of California wine is written it will derive from smaller studies of the state's winegrowing regions, studies based on contemporaneous, primary sources. My purpose in writing this work has been to provide just such a study for two of the state's important wine districts, the Santa Clara Valley and the Santa Cruz Mountains, two areas whose histories are at once distinct and intertwined.

The Santa Clara Valley was the home of Northern California's wine industry. The land today that presents a neat pattern of suburbanization was once a great sea of vines. This study traces the rise and decline of this great winegrowing district. And it attempts to show the sources for rebirth that have appeared during the Wine Revolution of the last twenty years. Of particular importance has been the rebirth of a fine premium wine industry in the surrounding Santa Cruz Mountains, an area that bottle for bottle probably produces the finest wine in North America. The history of these two areas seems worth the telling.

My approach in gathering historical data has been inductive wherever possible. I have tried to piece together a picture of the past from direct sources of the past. I have also tried to place this local history into the larger picture of the state's wine industry and the national economy. This has been a particularly important goal. I hope that the reader can understand the larger pattern of the state's wine history since there is no single work to which he can turn today for a systematic tracing of such a history from the earliest days to the present.

Most of the sources I have employed are readily available to the reader. The Bancroft Library on the Berkeley campus of the University of California has been my chief resource. For periodicals the San Francisco Public Library, the library of San Jose State University and the San Jose Historical Museum have been particularly useful. The California Room at San Jose Public Library is an indispensable source of local history materials for this area. Research papers on file at De Anza College's California History Center have provided a unique reference, based as they are so often on oral history resources.

I must also express my very special appreciation to a tireless group of wine and history lovers whose keen eyes and faithful scissors have provided me over the years with a continuous flow of local, wine related periodical data: Margaret Scott Dealey, Marie Thomason, Donald L. Gerber, Anne Teal Ryan, Dr. Loron N. McGillis and my mother, Charlene F. Sullivan. And for giving order to this potential jungle of material, as well as a special order particularly salutary to the life of a writer, I thank my wife, Rosslyn Polansky Sullivan.

Charles L. Sullivan

Los Gatos, California
November, 1981

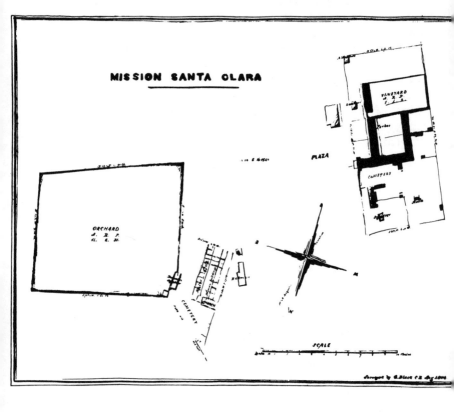

Nineteenth century map of Mission Santa Clara indicates vineyard site.

I. MISSION AND PUEBLO WINES AND VINES

The houses are pleasant . . . and
stand in the midst of orchards and hedges
of vines bearing luxuriant clusters of
the richest grapes.
— Otto von Kotzebue 1824

THE SETTING

The decision by Spanish authorities to advance their frontier of empire into Alta California was encouraged by the knowledge, partial as it was, that the geographical setting there was a good one, certainly less severe than that which the missions had faced in Baja California and along the Sonoran frontier. It was a land that could surely support a system of missions and presidial communities.

It did not take long for the padres and Spanish officials to realize, however, that the hoped for Mediterranean conditions were very much modified by coastal fogs, particularly during the warmer months of the growing season. Thus, it would be the coastal valleys, inland enough to ripen crops, but still favorably affected by the cooling breezes of a maritime influence, where the mission would be most successful as an almost self-sufficient agricultural community.

No physical setting better fit these conditions than the valley in which the Mission Santa Clara was founded in January of 1777. Later in that year, on November 29, a few miles to the east, the Pueblo of San Jose was established, the first civil settlement in Alta California.

For those padres, officials and settlers who knew something of Old Spain, it was not necessary to spend many years here to realize the close resemblance between this new land and many portions of Iberia. The climate was in many ways identical. There was a warm, dry summer, preceded by a fairly wet spring and winter. The growing season was rarely shortened by killing frosts. In short, what would grow well in Spain would probably do well here in the coastal valleys of Alta California. The valley's soils were rich and the water supply in the north seemed dependable.

1

There was never any question as to whether grapes would do well in this new land. Spanish explorers and early visitors noted right away the snarls of the native *Vitis californica* climbing the trees along the creeks and streams in the Santa Clara Valley and up into the surrounding foothills of the Santa Cruz Mountains. In fact, in the hills to the south and west of the main part of the valley the situation was so remarkable that they named the area "Uvas" for the wild grapes found growing there.

THE MISSION AND PUEBLO

The picture of mission viticulture and winemaking popularized over the years is often misleading. Writers on California wine have often led their readers to believe that the Franciscan fathers felt some compelling need to have wine made from grapes grown on their own premises to serve for the Mass. From this we are sometimes led to infer that they came up to Alta California armed with grape cuttings and began popping them into the ground within hours after raising the altar at the new mission. These dedicated men had far more important and trying tasks in the early days of their primitive establishments than to be much concerned about the source of wine for Mass. Survival and the spiritual success of their missions made such matters fade in importance. For some years wine was shipped up to the frontier from southern sources.

If there were any grape cuttings brought up by the pioneers who established the first mission at San Diego in 1769, none survived. They probably did not arrive in Alta California until 1778 or 1779 at Mission San Juan Capistrano. During most of the 1770s Father Serra was bringing wine and brandy into the province from Baja California and as late as 1781 he was still complaining to Father Lasuen about the shortages of altar wine. It is probable that California's first vintage year was 1782, the wine being produced by Father Pablo de Mugartogui at San Juan Capistrano.[1] Mission grapes were probably first successfully planted at the Santa Clara Mission in 1798 and the first wine was produced in 1802.[2]

It is clear that wine shipments from southern sources continued for years and all evidence points to a severe lag in winegrowing at the northern missions. When Captain George Vancouver visited California in 1792, he came down to the Santa Clara Mission and took care to bring along his own supply of wine and "grog." He and his naturalist found some clumsy starts being made at viticulture but

2

thought the failure lay in the padres' lack of practical knowledge. Later, in 1806, when the Russian visitor from Alaska, Nikolai Rezanov, came down to San Francisco Bay, he was served poor Baja California wine at Mission Dolores in San Francisco. But the naturalist, Georg von Langsdorff, crossed the bay and visited Mission San Jose, finding a good vineyard and a sound, sweet wine resembling a Malaga.[3]

But by the mid-1820s viticulture had finally become a successful part of Santa Clara Mission life. There was a flourishing little vineyard of something less than two acres under the care of Fathers Magin Catala and Jose Viader. By the 1830s there appears to have been grapes enough to supply part of the winemaking needs at Mission Dolores. In 1833 the American William Heath Davis tasted some of this San Francisco red wine from South Bay grapes and thought it excellent. Across the mountains at the Mission Santa Cruz the padres had a vineyard of 1210 vines, but there is no record of successful winemaking.[4]

By 1841, although most of the Santa Clara Mission lands had been taken out of the hands of the Church, the little vineyard with its 650 old vines was still well kept by the resident padre and his remaining Indian workers. The American naval officer Charles Wilkes visited the mission in that year and found the vineyard surrounded by a substantial wall with a gate always kept locked. During the summer and fall months, before the vintage, there was constant supervision to make sure that the ripening grapes were not stolen by the neophytes, who dearly loved their sweetness. It was a beautiful place, with vines trained up and headed in the Spanish style without trellis. For all of it, Wilkes thought the resulting wine pretty poor stuff.[5] Later, after the American conquest, the vineyard was expanded and became an important source of cuttings for local growers between 1849 and 1852.

The grapes brought north by the mission fathers were those they had known for years in Mexico and Baja California. They were clearly of European origin, but no sure counterpart in Europe has ever been identified. It is usual to generalize these pioneer varieties as Mission grapes, although the early American winegrowers more often termed them "California" or "native."

But there seem to have been three different varieties, at least in the early years. In Southern California one grape tended to produce a coarse, quite alcoholic wine, while the darker grape, more common in the north, produced a better table wine, with more color. We do not

3

know today why these differences were noticeable in the 1830s, but one thing we do know about both grapes. They produced a fairly coarse table wine when fermented dry, and when this baseness of character was combined with the padres' lack of winemaking talent, the result was often a catastrophe. The third type of grape found in the province was a Muscat, but we know little about it. No vine we have today can be identified with surety as having descended from the Mission Muscat.[6]

It did not take many years to discover that a better product resulted when the wine was fermented sweet. In fact, it was found that an even better product resulted when the fresh grape juice was not even fermented, but simply laced with a heavy dose of native brandy, the *aguardiente*. The alcohol was strong enough to retard any fermentation, and the retained sugar also acted as a preservative. This beverage was Angelica, California's first real contribution to winemaking. Of course, it was more a cordial than a wine. But it was found that long and careful barrel ageing produced a really superior drink. Many, however, would just as soon drink nothing but the young *aguardiente*, distilled from the white Mission wine in tiny copper pot stills found in most communities.[7]

The fathers at the Santa Clara Mission had not been happy that the new pueblo on the Guadalupe River had been established so close to their spiritual activities. They knew pueblo life nearby would make their task of Christianizing the Indians more difficult. It is a paradox that a major part of the demoralizing aspect of San Jose life came from the alcohol available there, much of which came from the crude wine and brandy made from vines developed from the cuttings that the settlers had received from the padres.

By the 1820s San Jose was a pleasant if dusty village of about 400, whose houses were surrounded by orchards and, according to a German traveler, had "hedges of vines bearing luxuriant clusters of the richest grapes." It was connected to Santa Clara by the Alameda, a beautiful tree-lined promenade.[8]

Everyone who could, had his own little vineyard and produced a crude wine that his family consumed during the months right after the vintage. The methods used to make this stuff were about the same as were practiced at most of the smaller missions. The crushing was done by foot, in a large receptacle, from which the resulting material could be drawn off. Sometimes cowhides were sewn together and a huge "vat" constructed by holding up the four corners with stout wooden poles. The result was drained off into any useful container available.

Earthenware crocks usually served well, as did any barrel or hogshead previously brought into the province bearing some kind of foreign liquor.

The fermentation was allowed to go apace, with the wild yeasts in the air and on the grape skins performing their functions. If a red wine was wanted the fermentation took place on the skins. Then they were pressed. If the juice was removed from the pulp and seeds right away during fermentation, a white wine resulted. "Brown" would be a more accurate adjective. A careful winemaker might rack the resulting stuff from one container to another and take off most of the resulting sludge that had developed at the bottom, but this would be rare in a home operation. The pulp that was left was then steeped in water and pressed again, the resulting liquid being then distilled into *aguardiente*.

In the pueblo there were a few of the little copper pot stills necessary, and a person owning one received a portion of what he distilled for anyone else. Also, if a particularly foul wine was produced, it would find its way into one of these stills.

From this description it is of little wonder that some men of intelligence and capital would have been moved to make money producing a potable commercial product from local grapes. Chief among these in San Jose was Antonio Maria Sunol. Born in Spain, he was thoroughly French, having served in the French navy. He jumped ship from the *Bordelais* at Monterey in 1818, married a daughter of the Bernal family and by 1823 was making and retailing wine in San Jose.

He acquired a good deal of land around the pueblo and, perhaps more important, his daughter Paula later caught the eye of a young Frenchman, Pierre Sainsevain, who came to Southern California in 1839 to help in the Los Angeles wine business of his uncle, Jean Louis Vignes. Sainsevain and his father-in-law had plenty of opportunity to assess the viticultural possibilities of the Santa Clara Valley and later were instrumental in their development.[9]

By the end of the 1840s, after the American conquest and the beginning of the Gold Rush, cool heads wondered at the great agricultural potential of this land. Almost everyone guessed that grapes would be a part of that future. The conclusions came primarily from viewing the climate and the soil, not from drinking the current product, certainly not that of the Santa Clara Valley. There was some drinkable wine being made in Southern California, and a good part of that found its way north to slake the alcoholic appetites of the Argonauts. We do not hear of commercial schemes to exploit the San

Jose product for this purpose. What was to be the pioneer wine industry of the Santa Clara Valley in the 1850s would at first depend on a local supply of cuttings from the ubiquitous Mission grape, but the pioneer winegrowers of the area would have nothing to do with the winemaking techniques of the Californio society that had preceded them into the valley. The most farseeing of these pioneers also understood that better grape varieties were necessary to take advantage of the remarkable environment of the valley.

Notes for Chapter I

Documentation for this work cannot be presented in its entirety and is primarily suggestive. Nevertheless, for subjects about which there has been significant controversy, a fairly full set of notes is supplied. Citations to contemporaneous materials are complete enough to insure the reader's ability to pursue the subject discussed.

1. Edith B. Webb, *Indian Life at the Old Missions* (Los Angeles, 1952), 95; Roy Brady, "The Swallow That Came from Capistrano," *New West* (September 24, 1979), 55-60; Hubert Howe Bancroft, *History of California* (San Francisco, 1884-1890), I, 641; Robert Archibald, *The Economic Aspects of the California Missions* (Washington DC, 1978), 165.

2. Herbert B. Leggett, "Early History of Wine Production in California," Master's thesis, History Department, University of California, Berkeley, 1939, 9.

3. Leggett, 10-11.

4. Irving McKee, "The First California Wines," *Wines & Vines* (April, 1947), 48; William Heath Davis, *Sixty Years in California* (San Francisco, 1889), 9, 304-5.

5. Charles Wilkes, *Narrative of the United States Exploratory Expedition . . .* (Philadelphia, 1845), V, 206-7; Bancroft, IV, 683.

6. Bancroft, VII, 46-7.

7. Brian McGinty, "Angelica," *Vintage* (October, 1975), 33-7; Thomas R. Hill, "California Angelica," *Wine & Vines* (November, 1980), 58-60.

8. Bancroft, II, 602.

9. Bancroft, IV, 135; V, 738; Irving McKee, "Historic Wine Growers of Santa Clara County," *California-Magazine of the Pacific* (September, 1950); Pierre Sainsevain to Arpad Haraszthy, June 22, 1886, with the "Haraszthy Family" manuscript, Bancroft Library, University of California, Berkeley; Irving McKee, "Jean Louis Vignes," *Wine Review* (July, 1948); San Jose *Evening News*, August 13, 1941.

Charles Lefranc arrived in San Francisco from Passy, France with goldrush immigrants. While visiting Valley's French populace, he selected a site for his New Almaden Vineyards and became the "Fa of local commercial viticulture. *(Almaden Collection)*

II. PIONEER DAYS — 1850-1879

*The whole valley of San Jose seems
one great garden . . . . In and around the
city are beautiful gardens and vineyards,
like modern Edens.*
— J.Q.A. Warren (1863)

BOOM TOWN

The story has often been told how towns of the coast emptied in the summer of 1848 after the news of the discovery up at Sutter's mill had been spread. San Jose was no exception. Statehood was soon to follow and the dusty little pueblo of previous years suddenly became a miniature boom town, the state's first capital. Passing through that summer, Walter Colton remarked that the area was "cultivated only in spots, but the immense yield in these is sufficient evidence of what the valley is capable." Dr. John Frost thought that "in a greater degree than any of the older towns of California, it has all the evidence of a thriving and progressive place." Hubert H. Bancroft later noticed, significantly, that the place had been filling up with foreigners, perhaps because of its aspirations to greatness. [1]

The main thoughts in the minds of local people during these hectic days, so far as agriculture was concerned, was how to take advantage of the soaring prices being paid in Northern California for things to eat. Some enormous profits were made from one season's work, but there was little thought of viticulture at first. Just about everyone had his litttle vineyard, some fairly large. But it takes several years from the planting of cuttings to the production of the first wine. Few had such patience.

Probably the most important thing that happened during the years 1849 to 1852, so far as this study is concerned, was a special demographic pattern that was taking place in the San Jose area. The valley was filling up with Frenchmen. In the years to come this fact would have a lasting effect on the history of the valley and on its agriculture. It would also leave a mark on the history of viticulture and winemaking for all of California.

Phillipe Prudhomme liquor store and saloon on Market Street, San Jose. Note the spigots on the casks from which the raffia covered bottles (top right) could be filled and refilled with wine. (*Mirassou Collection*)

"NEW ALMADEN VINEYARD,"

Near San Jose, California.

Ch. Lefranc, Proprietor.

New Almaden, named after its proximity to the quicksilver mines, is the oldest local commercial winegrowing establishment, dating from 1852. The farm shown above in the 1880's, included 150 acres of vines. The winery is still used for corporate offices and is located on Blossom Hill near Camden Ave., San Jose. (*Almaden Collection*)

The idea held by some that the Frenchman took no important part in the rush for California gold is inaccurate. By 1851 there were probably 25,000 French Argonauts in California, most of them concentrated at the diggings, with perhaps as many as 5,000 in San Francisco. The French consul's statistics mentioned only one other spot in California with any remarkable number of his countrymen, and this spot was San Jose. There were certainly no fewer than 1,000 here, perhaps 1,500. That Frenchmen should be attracted to California's golden riches is no surprise, and the political chaos in France between 1848 and 1850 must have cetainly encouraged some to look elsewhere for living space. [2]

A good look at conditions in Northern California in 1850 would naturally lead any Frenchman to consider San Jose as a place to choose for settlement. It was secure, stable and settled, and there was plenty of good land available. To this must be added the Sunol-Sainsevain connection, for the latter by now was a man with strong ties in southern and northern California and he understood thoroughly the agricultural potential of both regions. And his Francophile father-in-law had plenty of land to sell. Sainsevain's endorsement would certainly have counted with some, as did that of the French journalist Etienne Derbec, who passed through town in 1850 and wrote down what he saw. It was an ugly place for a state capital, but for agriculture, that was another matter. He predicted a fine future for the valley.

It is also probable that many Frenchmen coming to California were familiar with the general impression given French readers by previous Gallic visitors. They might not have read the work of Captain Jean Perouse, published in 1797, but its contents were part of the common image of California in France. The best travel book ever written on early California had come from the pen of another Frenchman, Count Eugene de Mofras, published in 1844. The picture he gave agreed with that of the naval officer. He said that California was a rich land inhabited by a backward people totally incapable of bringing forth its riches. It was a land simply begging for an energetic, enlightened people, such as the French. No place in the state better fit the picture drawn by these French writers than did the Santa Clara Valley.

Writers have previously noticed the French concentration in the South Bay and the Central European, mostly German, in the North Bay. Some have wondered at this pattern that obviously affected the future of the California wine industry. Part of the explanation lies in the fact that the French had a jump on the Germans. They headed for the best places available. In comparison to the Napa and Sonoma Valleys, in these earliest years, the Santa Clara Valley presented a picture of security and long established European culture. The northern counties were virtually on the wild frontier and a good part of the story there in the 1850s was colored by bloody and vicious Indian fighting.

It was natural that the earliest French settlers gravitated to the stability of the San Jose area, where Pierre Sainsevain's father-in-law was more than happy to sell them good land at quite reasonable prices. Sainsevain himself, more attached viticulturally to Southern California in the earliest days, was actually promoting the Santa Clara Valley by the end of the decade as a much better place than Los Angeles to raise wine grapes. He was correct.[3]

Between 1852 and the end of the decade from this body of French settlers there arose a small but important group of men who saw their future as nurserymen for the great agricultural gardens that were to develop in the coastal valleys of Northern California. A few brought some horticultural knowledge, but most simply saw a need and learned how to fill it. So far as winegrowing was concerned, they knew what good wine tasted like, they could tell that California could produce it, and they could easily see that what was being made here did not live up to the land's potential.

To this group of newcomers we must add a New England connection. Much of the early history of Northern California agriculture depended on the contribution of a very large number of experienced horticulturalists who came to the state after 1848 from New England. There was no special concentration of them in the Santa Clara Valley, but their presence was felt everywhere.

One can only marvel at the number of men who took leading positions in the early development of California agriculture and who had previously been members of the Massachusetts Horticultural Society. Colonel James L.L. Warren, the founder of the *California Farmer* and Frederick Macondray, the first president of the State Agricultural Society, stand foremost in a very long list of distinguished names, a large percentage of which are directly associated with the development of pioneer California winegrowing. Some of these New Englanders did come to the Santa Clara Valley, but more important to this study is their relationship with the French nurserymen here.[4]

California's agricultural history in the 1850s stands out as a period of searching and experimenting. So far as winegrowing was concerned, it was not a question of "whether?" but "where?" and "with what?"

New England sea captain Frederick Macondray brought vines to California from the East Coast in the 1850's notably the Zinfandel. He had close contacts with the San Jose nurserymen.

Charles Wetmore, head of the Board of State Viticultural Commissioners 1881-1890. This controversial person took a keen interest in the excellence of Santa Clara Valley wines and promoted especially the Westside (Mountain View, Cupertino, Saratoga, Los Gatos) region to the press and his peers.

The pages of the *Alta California* and the *California Farmer* pleaded throughout the decade for an advancement of the wine and grape interest in the state.[5] The call was for better wine and better wine grapes than the ordinary Missions. The nurserymen of San Jose answered the call.

THE NURSERYMEN

The French-New England connection of nurserymen became an important relationship that served to supply the earliest needs of Northern California vineyardists who wanted better wine grape varieties than the everpresent Mission. In time, direct importations from France and Germany were made by some of these pioneers, but for the moment New England would be the source. This important aspect of early California viticulture has been confused by claims asserted with conviction as to who imported what grapes to California first. The later commercial position of some of the claimants tended to color their perception of the past, and many historical writers trying to reconstruct the early years of California viticulture have too often gone to the literature of these special pleadings, written years after the event. In other words, instead of going to the materials of the 1850s, most writers have gone to the 1880s and after to acquire their primary sources of information.[6]

It is a well known fact that European *Vitis vinifera* were grown in a large number of varieties on Long Island and in New England as early as the 1820s. By the 1830s a veritable grape industry had grown up around Boston. Its purpose was to raise hothouse table grapes for the local "carriage trade." Many of the best varieties also made fairly good wine, but this fact was of little interest to the easterners.[7]

The first grape vines that came around the Horn after 1849 were primarily from these New England vinifera varieties. There were also several of the best American hybrids, such as Catawba, Isabella and Concord. A list of the New England varieties today would include many grapes mostly no longer known or appreciated. But we may recall some, such as the Black Hamburg, the Muscat de Frontignan or Muscat Blanc, Zinfandel, White Malvasia, Golden Chasselas and Muscat of Alexandria. Since these grapes were the first to arrive in California after the American conquest, it follows that some of the first examples of wine from *Vitis vinifera*, other than Mission, should be from them. By the end of the 1850s, however, the European imports of several San Jose nurserymen pushed a large number of these, but not all, into the background.

Antoine Delmas, San Jose's great French agricultural specialist in San Jose in the 1850's. With him are his two sons, Joseph and Delphin. His large nursery, called the "French Garden," was located in Santa Clara and carried the best early collection of foreign grapes in the state.

Antoine Delmas

So far as viticulture is concerned the master of the French nurserymen in San Jose was Antoine Delmas. In 1851 he purchased land in town from Antonio Sunol and in 1852 was the first to import European grape vines into the area and the state. His imports came both from France and New England, but tradition eventually had it that they all came from France, a very unlikely possibility when one sees all the standard New England vinifera varieties in his first nursery lists. But he was the first to import the better sort of wine grape from France and is now generally remembered for this event. By 1855 Delmas began a string of victories for his grape collections at competitions throughout Northern California that could be matched by no other person in the state.

Delmas's French Gardens won the first award for foreign grapes at the 1855 meeting of the California State Agricultural Society, but the varieties he exhibited indicate that his French imports were not yet in full bearing. Next year he had to settle for second place to Frederick Macondray, the New England sea captain responsible for bringing many of the first eastern vinifera varieties to California, including the Zinfandel.[8]

When Colonel James Warren visited San Jose, he pronounced the Delmas nursery "the *Premium* grape and wine Garden of San Jose," and went on to declare that the nursery vineyard was "by far the best in the state." In 1857, at the Santa Clara County Fair, Delmas was finally able to show off a few of his French imports under such names as "Cabrunet" and "Black Meunier." None of his fellow nurserymen had any varieties to show yet but Missions, eastern hybrids and the standard New England vinifera imports. From then until 1861 not a year went by without Delmas winning the lion's share of the grape awards at the state and county levels.[9]

Meanwhile Delmas took an active role in helping determine the best wine grapes for California. In 1857 he joined Louis Prevost and Thomas Fallon in providing the San Jose Pioneer Horticultural Society with a list of recommended varieties, many of which he had first imported himself. Those of later interest, presented in their pioneer spelling were for red wine: Barbaroux, Aramon, Black Gamet, Merleau, Le Meunier, Medoc, Le Teinturier, the Pineau and Black Hamburg. For white wine they suggested: White Tokai, White Coulombard, La Folle Blanche, Verdal, White Malvasia and White Morillon. That they suggested the Mission for making Champagne indicates something of their hopes, perhaps encouragement for

Stanford Winery as it stands today. Leland Stanford's Palo Alto Farm and Winery (built in 1888) were abruptly closed after University instruction commenced. David Starr Jordan, first president and ardent prohibitionist led the fight to make Palo Alto a dry town. It's ironic that a major portion of the University endowment was the largest vineyard in the world, the Stanford Vina Farm, Tehama County, that included 59,000 acres.

Jarvis brothers ad shows the extent of the company's marketing and production. Their large vineyard at Vine Hill above Scotts Valley is where the Smothers Winery is located today.

In the 1850's San Jose had the largest concentration of nurseries in the state. The Bernard S. Fox nursery was located next ot those of Joseph Aram and John Rock, just south of what is today the intersection of Shallenberger Road and 101. (*Thompson and West Atlas, 1876*)

19

Sainsevain's experiments, but little knowledge of viticulture or winemaking. They added rather nonchalantly, that "it is now a well established fact that we are in the very best wine country in the world." [10]

Of particular importance to California vineyardists was Delmas' 1859 introduction of the use of elemental sulfur to fight mildew. He also imported some of the first authentic European winery and distillery equipment into the state in 1860. [11]

Delmas also made wine commercially but never on a large scale. His chief interest seems to have been in testing certain vinifera varieties in the California environment. In this capacity he made his mark in history as one of the discoverers of the Zinfandel as a superior wine grape. At the time he did not realize the historical significance of his find, and only recently has it come to light. [12]

In his New England vinifera importations was a grape called the Black St. Peter's, which we now know to be virtually identical to the Zinfandel. He sold rooted cuttings of this vine and probably in 1856 sent some up to Mariano Vallejo in Sonoma, where they were planted in his vineyard. [13] In 1858 Delmas made a red wine in a claret style from the Black St. Peter's and the next year it was judged the best wine in California at the State Fair. The *Alta California* dubbed it a "fine French claret." The state committee that gave Delmas his award was confused by the fact that the wine was made from "foreign grapes that had been selected more as a table fruit than for winemaking." The same year the Zinfandel was introduced under its own name to the North Bay counties by way of New Englanders Macondray and J.W. Osborne, but it was already growing well in General Vallejo's vineyard. [14]

By the end of the 1860s the Zinfandel had won its place in California winemaking and by then all the Black St. Peter's vines in the Santa Clara Valley had magically changed into Zinfandel. Over a quarter of a century later the retired nurseryman reflected on the matter and pointed to J.P. Pierce's Santa Clara vineyard, well known for its Zinfandel. Delmas had grafted it over from Mission to Black St. Peter's in 1861. [15]

The direct New England connection in the Santa Clara Valley was Bernard S. Fox, formerly superintendent of Hovey & Co., Boston's leading nursery establishment. Fox had come to the United States from Ireland in 1848 and four years later accompanied a huge shipment of nursery stock from New England to California. In 1853 he and a partner formed the San Jose Valley Nursery and soon had it established on a large plot of land two miles north of town. Before long he had the greatest nursery garden in the area. According to Berkeley's Professor E.J. Wickson, Fox was "a quaint Irish bachelor gentleman, well trained in handling plants, with a fine thrift, a hunger for hard work and an acuteness in trade." [16]

Fox's gravestone has a pear on it, not a bunch of grapes, and rightly so. He is singled out here for his contribution to viticulture more for his New England connection and the support he gave the French nurserymen, than for the work he actually did in the field of viticulture. But he did push winegrowing and he stressed the importance of good *Vitis vinifera*. When the State Fair was held in San Jose in 1856 he rightly argued that New England vinifera did much better in the Santa Clara Valley under open air culture than they did in the East under glass. In 1857 his nursery had 86 different vinifera varieties, mostly from New England, Next year he raised the number to 122 and advertised his collection in the local press. [17]

The Pellier Brothers

Probably the presence of but two such men as Delmas and Fox would have been sufficient to have forwarded the interests of quality viticulture in these pioneer days here. But there were many more. One name stands out in this history, not so much for the proportions of the early work connected with it, but more for what came later. It is that of the brothers Pellier, Louis and Pierre. They too were encouraged to leave their homeland near La Rochelle by the political and social chaos there in the 1840s, and by the attraction of California gold. Between 1850 and 1854 Louis became a San Jose nurseryman entrepreneur and land developer, who apparently employed the services of his younger brother, Pierre, to bring cuttings and seeds from France to help stock the nursery. The exact nature of these importations and their date have been clouded by controversy and various family and local traditions which need not be examined in this study.

What is clear about the Pellier work in San Jose is that Louis' six acre nursery, the City Gardens, was one of the many in town and by the early 1860s was one of the most important. It is clear that certain French wine grape varieties were imported and collected at the nursery, and years later were so carefully maintained by Pierre that by the 1880s the so-called Pellier collection could still be considered intact, authentic and unique. It is also fairly clear from the lists of Pellier's nursery collections in the late 1850s that these imports were by no means so early as many have suggested. [18]

21

In the late 1850s Pierre worked for Louis in the nursery and together they built up the operation's stock and reputation. The grapevines in their vineyard were primarily New England vinifera table varieties. At the county fairs during these years they won many awards for their fruit but consistently had to take a back seat to the remarkable Delmas collections of vinifera grapes. They made some wine and by 1860 were producing excellent peach and pear brandy. In that year Pierre left the City Gardens and with his young and pregnant wife moved north to Mission San Jose to work at Clement Colombet's winery. [19]

Meanwhile Louis' nursery continued to gain prestige. In 1861 a correspondent of the *Alta California* stated that his, along with those of Delmas and Prevost, could "not be exceeded on this continent." Louis had about 4,000 vines in his vineyard now and had obtained good European vinifera, perhaps from a trip to Europe by Pierre in 1858. By 1863 Louis had 50 varieties for sale, including the "Melon Blanc," "Frank Rissling" and "Caburet." In 1863, J.Q.A. Warren visited the place and termed it "large and splendid." [20]

Meanwhile in 1861 Louis had made a very large commitment to viticulture by purchasing a large tract of land east of San Jose in the foothills of Evergreen. [21] He struck a deal with Pierre, who brought his family down to the new place, and by 1862 began planting vines taken from the City Gardens. By the mid-1860s the partnership between the brothers began to deteriorate, as did Louis' 1860 marriage. The rift became so deep between Louis and Pierre that they actually cut the family house in San Jose in two, and one half was carted out to Evergreen. By the end of the decade Louis' health and spirit had broken. He had separated from his wife and began selling off his town property. He died an unhappy man in 1872. Pierre then acquired title to the Evergreen property and proceeded to make it a viticultural showplace in the 1870s. When the great Wine Boom of the 1880s struck the Santa Clara Valley, Pierre Pellier was correctly hailed as one of the winegrowing pioneers of the area, although little was said of the important role played by Louis, who is today best remembered for his introduction of little French prune to the valley. [22]

There were many other pioneer nurserymen in the valley, French and otherwise, who made contributions to winegrowing. Louis Prevost, Delmas's friend and neighbor, had an important nursery vineyard, as did J.B. Bontemps. Over in the town of Santa Clara L.A. Gould was the master of the viticultural nursery work, winning a silver cup at the county fair in 1858 for his grape collection and the award for the county's finest vineyard in 1859. Over the years the bulk of the area's nursery business left the hands of the French pioneers and by 1873 Colonel Warren remarked that not one was still in operation. But in these earlier years they had a strong sense of professional and cultural identity. They held social gatherings and certainly did not stand aloof from their fellow non-Gallic nurserymen.

No better picture could be given of the group than that conveyed at a party given by the "Gardeners of San Jose" on August 30, 1855 at the Hotel de Bordeaux, in honor of the patron saint of horticulture. A great floral display stood at the head of the hall and in it could be seen the letters "F and A" to symbolize the friendly union of French and American nurserymen.

Major S.J. Hensley contributed some of his famous pears and Antoine Delmas brought a wide variety of table grapes. Prevost was in charge of apples and the Pelliers brought in peaches and some Isabella grapes. Pierre excited the company later in the evening when one of the gas lamps exploded over his head. A bevy of young ladies had a great time putting out the flames, and he finished the evening with his head wrapped in kerchiefs.

John Lewelling came down from Mission San Jose, bringing peaches and strawberries from his famed San Lorenzo nursery farther north. Captain Thomas Fallon was in charge of the melon detail.

They all got very happy drinking Los Angeles wine, most likely supplied by Pierre Sainsevain. They read poetry in French and English, with Prevost acting as interpreter when one was needed. They sang songs in French, Italian and English and rocked the hall with the strains of La Marseillaise. The party was still going at midnight when the local correspondent staggered out, loaded with fruit by M. Delmas for the "folks at home."[23]

THE PIONEER WINEMAKERS

A great change in the pattern of California life took place in the decades following the 1850s. Vigilance committees, armed confrontations between squatters and land owners, the wild and woolly adventures of the American conquest and early statehood had all become part of history. The hot-blooded roughneck with little but his horse, weapons and bags was now more often an established farmer/citizen, growing in wealth and enjoying the virtues and rewards of a stable family life and of law and order.

The railroad came and the land was cut up into smaller holdings. But extensive agriculture was still the rule through the 1860s and 1870s. The wine interest remained a minor part of the total scene, but it grew, doubling in size during each of the two decades. When the great Wine Boom took place in the 1880s, the pattern for what was to develop had already been established, even if its dimensions and importance had not.

By the end of the 1850s we begin to see a few small developments that indicate the beginnings of a tiny wine industry in the Santa Clara Valley and back in the Santa Cruz Mountains. If by some miracle a person had been able to fly over the valley at the start of the new decade, he would have been hard put to see the effects of the viticultural seeds planted by the men discussed above, for as yet winegrowing was not important in the area's total agricultural picture. Grain and livestock predominated, and would until the 1880s. But a very close look would have revealed a bit more than just the nurseries in San Jose and Santa Clara. There was obviously a market in California for wine and brandy, as can be seen from the huge imports during the 1850s. From 1853 to 1856 alone the young state brought in over four million gallons of foreign wine and three million gallons of brandy. There were some who were willing to take a shot at a portion of this market. [24]

Charles Lefranc

Charles Lefranc was the father of the commercial wine industry in the Santa Clara Valley. No myths, unproved legends, no mysterious enigmas or questionable family traditions surround his name or works. His influence on viticulture and wine making in the South Bay was deep and continuous from the 1850s until his accidental death in 1887. He was a hard nosed country winemaker, an important part of the area's French community and a very useful citizen, willing to sacrifice for the general improvement of his adopted land.

Lefranc came to San Francisco in 1850 and was soon attracted to the French community around San Jose. He used to come down on holidays with his friend Paul Verdier, later well known at San Francisco's City of Paris department store. He met a countryman, Etienne Bernard Edmond Thée, who had acquired a large piece of land south of town along Guadalupe Creek, a part of the Narvaez Rancho. In time Lefranc became enamoured of Thée's daughter, Marie Adele, and in 1857 they were married. Earlier Thée had determined to develop a vineyard at the northern end of the Almaden Valley and had purchased a wagon load of grape cuttings from the Santa Clara Mission. Tradition has it that he put them in the ground in 1852, but there is good reason to believe that 1851 is a more accurate date. [25]

Together Thée and Lefranc farmed the 350 acre tract and expanded

24

the vineyard to about 17,000 vines by 1858, Charles and Marie Adele now having acquired a half interest in the property. They made some ordinary wine from the Mission grapes and actually exhibited the grapes themselves at the 1857 San Francisco Mechanics Fair. But from the first Charles had not been satisfied with the product of Thée's vineyard. In 1857, perhaps as early as 1856, he sent home to France for a wide variety of good wine grape vines to plant in what he was then calling his "Sweet Grape Vineyard." He also sold them commercially, announcing in the San Jose *Tribune* that his May, 1858 imports derived "from the most celebrated Vineyards in France." So as to maximize the number of vines from this importation, Lefranc grafted single buds of the vinifera onto *Vitis californica* vines he found in profusion along Guadalupe Creek. Many of these grafted vines were still flourishing in the 1880s.[26]

By 1862 Lefranc's New Almaden Vineyard, named now for the great quicksilver mine in the hills behind his place, could boast 40,000 vines and from that year he claimed to have started making really good wine, since his French imports were now in full bearing. In the same year he acted as the county's representative to the state wine convention in San Francisco.

During the 1860s he expanded his operation to 75 acres of vines, while his little winery had grown to a capacity of 100,000 gallons. Year after year his wines won prize after prize at the county fairs, the best white, the best claret, best brandy, best sherry. This pattern continued through the 1870s. In 1869 Lefranc acquired the vines from Frank Stock's vineyard in San Jose, mostly German varieties that had been imported by Stock in 1859. Lefranc dug up the vines and hauled them out to New Almaden in wagons. There they became the basis for his excellent Rieslings that later won the highest praise from the great Charles Krug. In 1876 Lefranc built a larger winery and constructed a large number of redwood tanks.

Both Charles Wetmore, the viticultural commissioner and Professor Eugene Hilgard of the University of California, had much to say about Lefranc's winery and vineyard techniques.[27] Planting many of his vines on very close centers, he was able to increase the intensity of his wines' flavors, particularly noticeable in his Malvoisie, normally a fairly ordinary wine. His ports and Angelica had reputations for longevity and excellence, but it was his claret that brought the most praise from these experts. According to Wetmore, Lefranc's old Malbec vines were, before the 1880s, the only large plantation of good red Bordeaux vines in California. Sometimes, he thought, Lefranc let his grapes get overripe, but some of the Malbecs from the 1870s apparently were perfection. Hilgard was also impressed, particularly by the Frenchman's cellar techniques. He praised Lefranc's close supervision of his personnel and his emphasis on almost split second timing in performing specific cellar operations during and after fermentation.

Wetmore was particularly interested by Lefranc's collection of vines as one of the possible bases for the expansion of California's better wine varieties. But the Frenchman was too casual in his approach for the scholarly commissioner. Cabernet Sauvignon was mixed in with the Malbec. Some vines had been misnamed for years. Wetmore's orderly mind was actually offended and he was particularly perturbed by the fact that Lefranc didn't seem to share his concern. Wetmore liked Pierre Pellier's collection for its order, but for quality and depth Lefranc's was tops. [28]

The fact is that Charles Lefranc was a primitive, so far as viticulture and winemaking were concerned, but he watched others, studied the state of the art, experimented with little concern for established tradition, and year in and out he produced a product that convinced others of the potential excellence of Santa Clara Valley wines. Charles Lefranc made the New Almaden Vineyard a commercial success and struggled through the economic depression of the 1870s when many others threw in the sponge. He made excellent wine and everyone knew it and praised him for it. He served as a model and gauge for others. The deference shown him by others in the valley and the state was obvious and sincere. His attitude to it was usually one of mild amusement. He would have nothing to do with honorific offices and consistently argued that he had nothing to give others in the way of knowledge, save the manifest examples of his own practical experience.

Lefranc was the picture of continuity. He and his wife raised their family and lived a good life on the bank of the Guadalupe. By the 1870s the place was a paradise of trees, flowers and vines. Many of the pepper trees he planted still grace the old homestead on Blossom Hill Road. A visitor's comments give us a pretty picture of life at New Almaden Vineyard. [29]

> The large, cheerful farm buildings are upon a gentle rise of ground above the area of vines, which is nearly level. An Alsacian foreman showed us through the wine cellars. A servant-maid bustling about the yard was a thorough French peasant, only lacking the wooden shoes. The long tables, set for the forty hands employed in the vintage time,

LONE-HILL VINEYARD, SEVEN MILES SOUTHWEST OF SAN JOSE, CAL. D. M. HARWOOD, PROPRIETOR.

155 ACRES IN VINES.   220 ACRES IN RAN[...]

David M. Harwood's Lone Hill Vineyard was the largest in the county in the 1860's, formerly located north of Harwood and Blossom Hill Roads.

27

were spread with viands in the French fashion. Scarcely a word of English was spoken . . . . One feels very much abroad in such scenes on American soil.

Lone Hill and the Foothill District

Lefranc's success attracted others to the land bordering the southern foothills of the valley. Before the end of the 1860s the land north and west of his property had developed into the valley's foremost viticultural district. Isaac Branham had lived there for some time on the road that today bears his name. In 1861 he put in a 50 acre vineyard. By 1865 he was producing about 5,000 gallons of wine. For neighbors he had the Stockton brothers, Stephenson and Dr. N.H., who followed suit with two vineyards that eventually totaled over 100 acres. The Doctor's bore the name Live Oak Vineyard and the other was called Gravel Ridge Vineyard. N.H. Stockton later built a good stone cellar and maintained a retail sales room in San Jose for a few years.

Lefranc's most important new neighbor was County Assessor David M. Harwood who in 1865 planted a 40 acre vineyard on the south side of Lone Hill along what is today Harwood Road, north of Blossom Hill Road. Little can be seen of Lone Hill today, as it has long since been quarried down. He expanded his planting yearly until his was for a while the largest vineyard in the valley, with 115 acres in 1868. By 1871 he was producing over 20,000 gallons of wine per year from his grapes which included Folle Blanche, Black Burgundy and Riesling. The Lone Hill Vineyard passed into the hands of Christian Freyschlag in the 1880s, but its name remained with the land. [30]

We might say that this district lay in a crescent extending west of the Almaden Road and parallel to the course of Guadalupe Creek as it flowed from the hills just west of Lefranc's place. Some called it the "Foothill District," but the term did not stick. In its natural state it was a land of oak trees and poison oak vines, on a reddish, gravelly clay and loam soil. It tended to have a slight elevation, due to the drainage pattern in that part of the valley, and this, along with other factors, freed vineyardists from much of the anxiety associated with heavy spring frosts. This was part of what would later be called the valley's thermal belt. Small vineyards also sprang up in the Almaden Valley and to the west towards Los Gatos and what would be Saratoga. By the end of the decade the San Jose *Mercury* estimated that wine production in the area was over 75,000 gallons.

Most of this wine did not leave the valley. It was sold by the barrel or half barrel at the winery or in San Jose or in outlying communities in grocery stores, right from the barrel into the buyer's container. This was an important part of life to many inhabitants of the valley and surrounding hills, particularly those of French descent. But drinking wine as a healthy part of a daily diet soon caught on here and with many more than just those of Latin extraction. It was respectable and only the most rigid who lived here totally abstained from making this country wine a part of their lives. Some winegrowers sold their products outside the area, but this would not be a regular aspect of the local industry until the 1880s.

Pierre Sainsevain

This California pioneer's relationship to the early days of Southern California wine making has already been discussed. And his role in the San Jose settlement of large numbers of early French people may have been critical. Nevertheless, he eventually settled permanently in the San Jose area and for many years was one of the town's most respected winegrowers.

In 1847 Antonio Sunol acquired the 2219 acre Rancho de los Coches to the west of town and gave Pierre and his daughter Paula a third of it in 1849. (He kept a third for himself and sold the rest to Henry Naglee.) Sainsevain lived in San Jose until 1855 and then worked on his wine interests in Southern California. He sold off part of his land, a 55 acre plot to Captain Stefano Splivalo, who planted a 20 acre vineyard on it. What was finally left was a ranch Pierre called Sainsevain Villa, 116 acres in size.

Sainsevain replanted some of his old vineyard to good vinifera varieties and by 1865 was making about 6500 gallons of red table wine each year. His claret won the award for the best red wine at the County Fair in 1868, Lefranc winning the white wine category. Sainsevain called his vineyard Belle Vue and marketed his wines in San Jose under the trade name "Menlo Park." By 1870 his production was up to 20,000 gallons. But during the next four years he began selling off pieces of the Villa and in 1874 closed down his wine operations and went to Central America on

Alexander Montgomery, the patriarch of Cupertino's business establishment in the late 19th century, operated a small prune brandy distillery near the Crossroads.

another business venture.

In the 1880s Sainsevain returned to San Jose, taking up winemaking on a small scale and producing batches of fairly good sparkling wine, much better than his "Sparkling California" of the 1850s. He even invented a steam driven stemmer-crusher in 1882, which apparently was a success. When Paula, his wife, died in 1889 Pierre returned to France to live until his death in 1904 at the age of 85. [31]

There were other important winegrowers close to town. Frank Stock developed a good reputation for white wine made from his own imported German varieties, White Riesling, Franken Riesling (Sylvaner) and Traminer. South of town were J.E. Brown's Ridge Vineyard and the vineyards of Dr. B.F. Cory and William Buck. To the east of town Victor Speckins and John Auzerais had good spreads. Other names indicate the multi-national character of wine grape growers around San Jose: Muller, Brohaska, Kennedy, Moody, Spencer, Reed, Prati, Guerin, Flury, Spencer, Rawley. In the town of Santa Clara, the old mission vineyard was now part of the College and had been expanded to four acres. Mr. Gould's vineyard and nursery were predominant in Santa Clara for some years, but later R.T. and J.P. Pierce became the most important winegrowers. Others of note were William Lenk, James Lawry and William Thomburg.

West of town, near today's Steven's Creek, there was little viticulture in early years. An exception was a tiny spot of Mission grape vines, four acres in size, planted by the old pioneer Elisha Stephens. When civilization started to move out that way, the captain of the party that opened the California Trail in 1844 moved on to the Bakersfield area.

Henry M. Naglee

While the roots of a local wine industry were being set outside town, something quite different in regard to winemaking was going on in San Jose. By the 1870s this community was to become the brandy making capital of California, not because so much was produced, but because of what was made by one maker. This brandy maker was General Henry Morris Naglee, a Civil War veteran who had seen action in California during the Mexican War and had later bought land with his inherited wealth in several places around San Jose. He first purchased land in 1852 and moved here in 1858. He was happy to rush off to the Civil War, as much to get away from an entangling love affair as anything else.[32]

After the war he returned with a very much altered view of his viticultural future. He had been to France twice, visiting Cognac and studying brandy making in depth. On his return to San Jose he began grafting over much of the vineyard he had planted on the east side of town to good wine varieties and in 1868 built his winery and distillery.

A terrible fire in 1869 set him back in his plans but by the mid 1870s he was selling a kind of brandy unheard of before on either side of the Atlantic. Some French ideas he accepted. Others he thought were nonsense. He believed that the best brandy would come from good wine made from top grade wine grapes. He despised most Mission brandies and would have nothing to do with the French Folle Blanche popular in Cognac. He wanted a part of his brandy flavor to be reminiscent of the grape variety employed. He made his from White Riesling, Charbono and a clone of the Pinot Noir.

His brandy was crystal clear, picking up no color to speak of in its ageing process, never receiving any kind of coloring additives. To effect this he aged his product in large 800 to 1500 upright Canadian and Indiana oak casks whose staves had been thoroughly steamed. He employed a continuous still of his own design that produced 170 gallons per day. A brandy historian has written that Naglee's ideas on style and some of his techniques made him "a harbinger of the modern brandy industry."[33]

The General experimented for years and was still doing so when he died in 1886. Meanwhile his brandies had carved a special place for themselves in the history of wines and spirits. He won an almost continuous string of awards and medals, not that it was so much like the French standard but because it was so good. The French themselves were amazed at this "white lightning" he produced. But they praised its "rare quality." At the Centennial Exposition in 1876 his "Naglia" won a special award as the "only American brandy on exhibit that approached the fine French spirits in flavor." Professor Eugene Hilgard, a constant thorn in the side of producers of mediocre California wines and brandies, rated Naglee's Burgundy Brandy 100 on a scale of 1-100. The General's Riesling Brandy received an 85, while California brandy in general got a 26.

It is difficult to evaluate the best wines of California a hundred years later. Brandy is another matter. When it is great it lasts and there was still Naglee Brandy around in the 1940s. A.R. Morrow thought it a totally superior product, as did the critic Robert Mayock of Los Amigos Winery fame.[34]

Naglee's personal reputation was nowhere nearly so good as that of his brandy. He had been continually in hot water with his superiors during both wars and his relations with women were the talk of the town. But he built a beautiful home on his grounds between 11th Street and Coyote Creek and surrounded it with one of the grandest gardens in the "Garden City." It was a park covering several acres and was open to the public on Sundays. Naglee was noted for never having been seen smiling, but he must have chuckled in 1883 when a temperance group visiting the State Teachers College in Ssan Jose asked to see Naglee Park. He invited them over and after the tour presented them with a fine buffet and punch. The latter was a lemonade well laced with the crystal clear Naglee brandy. The folks had a jolly time, some needing help to get out to the waiting carriages. It is little wonder that the General had to wait a quarter of a century after his death for a memorial to be raised in his memory. [35]

After he died in 1886, Naglee's daughters took over the estate, ceased brandy production, and slowly sold off the ageing vintages. These sales went on for over twenty years and helped keep up the reputation of "Naglia." His estate was eventually cut up and sold for town lots.

THE SANTA CRUZ MOUNTAINS

The mountains to the west of the Santa Clara Valley today produce some of the finest wines in North America. These Santa Cruz Mountain wines have a long history and their excellence is no modern phenomenon. In fact, far more land was planted to wine grapes almost a century ago than are to be found there today. These mountains, so close to the metropolitan Bay Area, have had a somewhat secluded history. They are fairly rugged and in some places look down over 2,000 feet on the valley below and on the Monterey Bay to the west. As a viticultural district this mountain area supplied a rather unique combination of soils and climate which has produced, in the minds of many connoisseurs, wines of elegant distinction. Cool nights, warm days above the surrounding fogs, shallow soils on rugged hillsides, and, most important, an almost fanatic, idealistic devotion by the winegrowers to their craft. These have combined to produce a distinctive history, at once an extension of the Santa Clara Valley's, but in a way separate and singular.

As was the case in the valley, but even more so here, winegrowing in these mountains developed in several fairly distinct districts, separated by rough landscape. These early districts have come to define, to some extent, the patterns of winegrowing here today. It must be noted that this mountain area contains portions of three different counties, Santa Clara, Santa Cruz and San Mateo. This fact tends to confuse the statistical picture so far as Santa Clara County is concerned, since there is no way to separate its figures into mountain and valley vineyards.

The outside world began discovering the mountain area near and below the summit between Santa Cruz and Los Gatos in the late 1850s, so far as viticulture was concerned. Vineyardists started winning awards at the Santa Clara County Fairs and San Francisco newspapers began to discover the area's possibilities. By 1866 the *Alta California* had sent a correspondent down to look things over and he discovered wine being made near the summit that would be a "formidable rival" for the valley winemakers; it was "of a grade unlike any yet presented." He wondered why some people in the wine trade didn't examine the possibilities for commercial planting here. But the capitalists did not pick up on such ideas until the 1880s. [36]

Viticulture actually had got its start in the mountains long before this. Lyman J. Burrell had moved up near the summit in 1853 and the next year his wife wrote home about all the good things they had growing, including their grape vines. Next year she thought that the area would be a very good place "for raising fruit, especially grapes." For a while people tried just about everything, but it would be fruit that would be the agricultural mainstay of the region after the lumbermen had cleared an area. By 1859 Burrell was exhibiting his grapes in San Jose and in the 1860s developed a little vineyard with no less than 29 different vinifera varieties. His son-in-law, Hiram C. Morrell, also settled near the summit and planted a vineyard in 1867. Their neighbor, Charles Henry McKiernan, was chiefly in lumber and orchards, but also had a good vineyard. "Mountain Charley" was better known for his battles with the grizzly bears in the early days, but later he became an important factor in the growth of the wine industry in San Jose. [37]

As important as the work of these men was, they were not so influential as winegrowers as they were as general vineyardists, who also grew great table grapes and sold their wine grapes to others. The winegrowing pioneers were the Jarvis brothers, down the hill toward Santa Cruz, and Dennis Feeley near the summit.

John W. and George M. Jarvis came overland to Oregon in 1853 and entered the Santa Cruz Mountains a few years later. Tradition has it that John Jarvis planted his first plot of Mission grapes near Vine

Hill in 1858, but the main planting was established in 1863 on his estate, called Vine Hill Rancho. There were 50 acres and eventually over 20 varieties planted on the slopes at the 1200 foot elevation. By the end of the decade the Jarvis wines had won a good reputation and the little winery was making about 20,000 gallons per year. By 1872 the total had reached 30,000 gallons at what they now were calling Mt. Vineyard Hill. By now the entire area had taken on the name Vine Hill, which it retains to this day. It was producing about half the wine being made in Santa Cruz County. Jarvis also began making brandy in the 1870s, using a double distilling process and employing small copper pot stills. In many ways the Jarvis brandy was like General Naglee's, particularly their "Reisling" brandy, which really made the Jarvis name known in California winemaking circles. In 1879 John again expanded his operations by planting his Union Vineyard, 63 acres of top notch wine grapes. George would soon move the center of their operations to San Jose in the 1880s. [38]

Dennis Feeley never attained the vast commercial success of the Jarvis brothers, but his personal prestige and his leadership were unsurpassed in the area. As a viticulturist he probably had no equal in California and as a winemaker he won plaudits across the nation. His Lexington Vineyard near the summit was planted to the very best European varieties by the early 1860s, before most others knew of anything much better than the Mission variety. Colonel Warren discovered Feeley's grapes in 1867 and in a few years had to admit that they were the best he had ever seen, anywhere.

During these early years Feeley had only 13 acres, but his varieties were the best. He stressed white wines, particularly Riesling, Sylvaner and Grey Riesling. His clarets were also famous, both Charles Krug and Frederic Pohndorff singling them out for special praise. Feeley's white varieties derived from Frank Stock's import to San Jose in 1859. Thomas Hart Hyatt was particularly taken by his Sylvaner. Years before the railroad came to the mountains he hauled his wines down to the valley by wagon and sold them east himself, refusing to compete, he said, with the "concocted stuff" of the San Francisco wine merchants. He eventually established a good trade in the New Orleans market. Feeley made wine into the 1890s until he was forced to retire when he began to grow blind. [39]

The mountain region to the north and west of the Summit/Vine Hill area also had a few glimmerings of viticultural activity between 1860 and 1879, but it was nowhere nearly so important. Out toward Bonny Doon and on Ben Lomond Mountain John Burns and Louis

Martin, among others, planted small vineyards. There were also a few places planted in the Congress Springs and Mt. Eden districts, but their real growth would be in the next decade. In the hills northwest of Saratoga in 1863 William Pffeffer bought land from Frank Gubser, on which he would eventually plant one of the first premium vineyards in the area. The Montebello district to the north would not really open up until the 1880s, but below the Ridge in the foothills around Stevens Creek Canyon, the Jesuits at Santa Clara College bought 160 acres of land in 1871 and planted vineyards to augment their wine supply. In 1875 they constructed a small winery and established the area as a religious retreat. They called it Villa Maria. The local folks called it Fathers' Villa.[40]

Farther to the north between 1853 and 1856 in San Mateo, Colonel Agoston Haraszthy, later to be famous for his pioneer viticultural efforts in Sonoma Valley, had tried to grow wine grapes near what is today the northern Crystal Springs reservoir. They did not do well because of the cool weather and fog. Successful winegrowing began somewhat farther south in the Woodside-Searsville area, near the Portola Valley, when Domenico Grosso planted a vineyard of wine grapes in the 1870s. Dr. Robert Tripp probably made the best wine in the area. He had established his famous Woodside Store in 1854 and planted a five acre vineyard in the early 1870s, making wine which he sold in bulk and under his own label, with the designation "San Mateo County Pioneer." This area, like most of the Santa Cruz Mountains above the Summit/Vine Hill districts, had to wait until the 1880s for serious winegrowing to get under way.[41]

Between 1860 and 1879 Santa Clara Valley and Santa Cruz Mountain winemakers had to face up to the natural and economic facts of life, so far as viticulture was concerned. They learned soon that powdery mildew could be a real problem but that it could be controlled by applying elemental sulfur. Frost was another matter valley vineyardists had to learn to live with, particularly those freezes that descended on them in April and May, burning back the new spring growth. Most of the valley was devastated by such a frost in 1867, but at this early date in viticultural history the vineyardist's best technique for combatting such assaults was prayer, although it did help to have your vines planted along the thermal belt or in the mountains.

In regard to economic problems, it is no secret that overexpansion of productive capacity was a major theme in 19th century American agricultural and industrial history. The situation was certainly not unknown to the California vineyardist in the late 1860s and mid 1870s. It was the old story of good prices, a rush to plant vines by too many people who did not know what they were doing, and then too many grapes, often of poor quality. But the moderate size of the local industry and its dependence on the local market as the major outlet of its product did tend to ameliorate the situation here. Other parts of the state were not so fortunate. Vines pulled up in Napa and Sonoma Valleys in the mid 1870s were instructive for local growers and prospective vineyardists. By the end of the 1870s there were a little more than 3,000 acres of vines in the area and the wine product was yet but a little more than 100,000 gallons. By the end of the next decade this product would be measured in the millions of gallons. The horrors of a really great depression still lay ahead for the local winegrower.

Taxes were another problem that plagued winemakers who also produced brandy and sweet wines. A federal tax left over from Civil War days was kept on spiritous products at a rate that made brandy makers howl for years. The chief howler was, of course, General Naglee. But a solid cut in the tax and on the method of its collection did bring some relief to this sector of the industry in 1877.[42]

Finally to be considered was a problem that continually faced the Santa Clara Valley vineyardist. It was, what grape varieties were best suited to the environment and make the best wine? What varieties would give the valley a distinct wine personality, such as was developing in the Napa and Sonoma Valleys and would soon evolve in the Livermore Valley?

Everyone seemed to agree that the Mission had to go, yet there were still hundreds of acres of this mediocre variety in the valley in 1879. Newcomers, who usually knew nothing about viticulture, and even less about wine quality, would too often decide on the variety to plant by using nothing more than pencil and paper. They used the figures paid for last year's crop and multiplied this figure by the estimated yield per acre. Which grape variety would win here between the Mission and the shy bearing Cabernet Sauvignon? All too often valley planters opted for the Malvoisie, Charbono and Mission.

Probably the greatest tragedy was the early attraction to the Charbono as an alternative to the Mission, and the slow acceptance of the Zinfandel as a far better choice. Charbono can be made into good wine on well drained, upland soils, but if grown on the valley floor it is heavy and rough. Years went by with this or that red variety enjoying a moment of popularity. Pellier and others called for the planting of Burgundy type grapes, but they were never properly identified. Years later viticultural experts would shake their heads at the widespread planting of Charbono by those who had been told that the "Charbonneau" was a top notch Burgundy varietal. Some persons even referred to it as Santa Clara Cabernet. Too many poor and mediocre grapes filled too many vineyards.

A man like Lefranc could do right well with his Malbec, Mataro and Riesling, even give away cuttings to those who would take them. But why should anyone take such advice? A simple calculation showed that these varieties were not as profitable as Malvoisie and Chasselas. There was not a strong sense of leadership among the pioneer winegrowers. In the northern counties Germans like Krug, Schram, Dresel and Bundschu browbeat their neighbors into planting better vines to upgrade the reputation of their district. Here the voices were not loud enough, and if some heard, not enough followed along. But in the mountains to the west the focus on premium varieties was much sharper.

We come to the end of the 1870s ready to observe the explosion that was to transform the wine interest here into a real industry. By now the picture of ethnic heterogeneity was clear. Lefranc, Naglee and Pellier were still dominant names, but a host of new faces were just offstage. As yet no clear focus on wine style was in sight. But no less than Arpad Haraszthy had declared that Santa Clara and Santa Cruz Counties were making the best wine in the state, even if the average gallon was not so good. Charles Wetmore insisted that the best collection of French vinifera varieties could be found here, confused as it was. The stage was set for the great Wine Boom.

Notes for Chapter II

1. John Frost, *History of the State of California* (Auburn, New York, 1851), 109.
2. Abraham P. Nasatir, *A French Journalist in the California Gold Rush* (Georgetown, California, 1964), 15, 26, 194-5.
3. San Jose *Telegraph,* December 30, 1857.
4. Charles L. Sullivan, "An Historian's Account of Zinfandel in

California," *Wines & Vines* (February, 1977), 18-20; Walton E. Bean, "James Warren and the Beginnings of Agricultural Institutions in California," *Pacific Historical Review* (December, 1944), 361-75; Marshall P. Wilder, *The Horticulture of Boston and Vicinity* (Boston, 1881), 49-50; *Transactions of the Massachusetts Horticultural Society* (Boston, 1834), 22; (1839), 29.

5. *Alta California,* hereafter *Alta,* 2/20/1851, 11/23/1854, 9/2/1857; *California Farmer,* hereafter *Farmer,* 12/7/1854, 1/11/1855, 3/22/1855.

6. Charles L. Sullivan, "A Viticultural Mystery Solved," *California History (California Historical Quarterly)* (Summer, 1978), 115-19.

7. Leon Adams, *The Wines of America,* 2nd Edition, (New York, 1978), 555; William Robert Prince, *Treatise on the Vine* (New York, 1830); J. Fiske Allen, *A Practical Treatise on the Culture and Treatment of the Grape Vine* (Boston, 1848).

8. *Farmer,* 10/17/1855, 10/10/1856; *Pacific Wine and Spirit Review,* 2/28/1903, hereafter *PWSR.*

9. *Telegraph,* 10/14/1857; *Alta,* 9/25/1858, 10/11/1859; *Transactions of the California State Agricultural Society, 1859* (Sacramento, 1860), 303; *1861,* 107-23, hereafter *Transactions.*

10. *Telegraph,* 5/19/1857; *Alta,* 9/11/1859.

11. *Alta,* 8/22/1860; *Farmer,* 11/9/1860.

12. Adams, 554-6; Sullivan, "Viticultural Mystery," 121-3. The idea that Agoston Haraszthy first imported the Zinfandel to California has been thoroughly discredited.

13. *Pacific Rural Press,* 9/30/1882, hereafter *PRP:* Charles L. Sullivan, "Black St. Peter's, Zinfandel Same?" *Wine Spectator* (November 16, 1979).

14. Allen, 308, 311; T. Hart Hyatt, *Hyatt's Handbook of Grape Culture* (San Francisco, 1876), 210; *Transactions, 1859,* 303; San Francisco *Evening Bulletin,* 5/1/1885; *California Wine, Wool and Stock Journal* (June, 1863), 107.

15. San Jose *Daily Herald,* 5/20/1885.

16. E.J. Wickson, *California Nurserymen and the Plant Industry, 1850-1910* (Los Angeles, 1921), 23-4.

17. *Farmer,* 10/10/1856.

18. *Farmer,* 11/21/1856, 10/9/1857; *Telegraph,* 10/14/1857, 11/13/1858.

19. Clyde Arbuckle, "Louis Pellier Nursery Lot," typescript, California Room, San Jose Public Library; Louis A. Pellier, *A True Account of the Introduction of le Petite d'Agen French Prune*...(San Jose, 1931); *Telegraph*, 9/23/1857, 10/14/1857; *Alta*, 9/27/1858, 8/14/1860.

20. San Jose *Mercury*, 9/13/1863; *California Wine, Wool and Stock Journal* (June, 1863), 99.

21. A plaque in Evergreen today commemorates this event, but inaccurately dates it as 1854.

22. Arbuckle, 2-3, 13-15; Interviews by the author of Marie Mirassou, widow of Herman Mirassou, a grandson of Pierre Pellier, September, 1979; Santa Clara County Recorder's Deed Books: 0-661, 27-15, 28-638, 23-81.

23. *Telegraph*, 9/11/1855; San Jose *Semi-Weekly Tribune*, 9/12/1855.

24. Bancroft, VII, 114.

25. *Mercury*, 6/4/1874; Kevin Starr, *Americans and the California Dream* (Oxford, 1973), 372.

26. Santa Clara County Recorder's Deed Book J-292; *Farmer*, 9/18/1857; *First Annual Report of the Board of State Viticultural Commissioners* (Sacramento, 1881), 48.

27. Eugene W. Hilgard was appointed Professor of Agriculture at the University of California in 1874. For 32 years he served the agricultural community as the leading advocate of the practical application of science on the California farm. He fostered the diea that the agricultural faculty should take their findings into the field and encouraged the development of agricultural experiment stations throughout the state.

28. *Mercury*, 11/4/1875; *PWSR*, 1/4/1884; 3/27/1885; *Second Annual Report of the Chief Executive Officer of the Board of State Viticultural Commissioners* (Sacramento, 1884), 39-40, 108-9, 112, 126.

29. William Henry Bishop, *Old Mexico and Her Lost Provinces* (New York, 1883), 359.

30. *Mercury*, 6/29/1865, 11/11/1866, 7/19/1866, 6/11/1868, 9/21/1871, 6/4/1874.

31. Clyde Arbuckle, *Santa Clara County Ranchos* (San Jose, 1968), 22; Frances L. Fox, *From Land Grant to Land Mark* (San Jose, 1978), 23-43; *Alta*, 8/8/1860; *Mercury*, 10/8/1868; San Jose *Times*, 10/11/1882; Irving McKee, "Jean Louis Vignes," *Wine Review*

(July, 1948); Sainsevain to Haraszthy, 6/22/1886.

32. The "amorous Naglee," as Bancroft called him, was something of a womanizer. One jilted lady published a book of his love letters and another won a judgement against him for breach of promise. Susan Fischler, "Wine, Women and Naglee," Studies in Local History, Leland High School, San Jose, California, 1977.

33. *Alta*, 2/24/1872; Thomas Hardy, *Notes on Vineyards in America and Europe* (1885), reprinted in *W&V*, 9/1967-9/1968; *W&V*, 3/77.

34. *Alta*, 2/19/1877; *Times*, 4/15/1881; *Mercury*, 4/17/1879; *W&V*, 7/1941; San Jose *Evening News*, 11/3/1944.

35. Donald C. Biggs, *Conquer and Colonize* (San Rafael, 1979), 81-113, 211-215; Helen W. Kennedy (ed.), *Vignettes of the Gardens of San Jose de Guadalupe* (San Francisco, 1938), 41-2; *Times*, 9/11/1883; *Wine Spectator*, 2/16/1981.

36. *Farmer*, 10/7/1859; *Alta*, 8/14/1866.

37. Reginald R. Steward (ed.), *The Burrell Letters* (Oakland, 1960), 39-44; Stephen Payne, *A Howling Wilderness* (Cupertino, 1978), 73-77, 101-116; *Alta*, 8/26/1860; *Farmer*, 10/13/1870; *Mercury*, 10/17/1867; *Tribune*, 10/28/1859.

38. Edward S. Harrison, *History of Santa Cruz County, California* (San Francisco, 1892), 180, 326; Edward Martin, *History of Santa Cruz County, California* (Los Angeles, 1911), 106; *PRP*, 1/20/1872; *Farmer*, 10/23/1873; *Alta*, 10/16/1872; *Redwood Rancher*, 7/1980.

39. *Farmer*, 10/17/1867; *Mercury*, 5/28/1874; *Times*, 12/18/1884; *Herald*, 4/13/1885; Hyatt, 148.

40. Mike Holland, "The Bonny Doon Grape War," *Santa Cruz Weekly* (March 11, 1981); Santa Clara County Recorder Deed Book R-207; Gerald McKevitt, *The University of Santa Clara* (Stanford, 1979), 97-98.

41. Gilbert Richards, *Crossroads* (Woodside, 1973), 105-6; Charles L. Sullivan, "A Man Named Agoston Haraszthy," *Vintage* (March, 1980), 23.

42. *Mercury*, 3/8/1877.

Exterior view of Prudhomme's wine and liquor store. Note the sign, lower right promoting "bar in rear, all California wines." (*Mirassou Collection*)

43

III. THE GREAT WINE BOOM

> *At this date Santa Clara and Santa*
> *Cruz Counties can show wines which have*
> *no superiors in California.*
> *— Arpad Haraszthy (1880)*

The American economy in the 1870's had suffered from a serious industrial and agricultural depression. Meanwhile between 1867 and 1875 California wine production had risen steadily and had, by the middle of the decade, far exceeded local consumption. The result had been much suffering among the state's winegrowers, less so in the Santa Clara Valley than most places. But at the same time the phylloxera root louse had begun its rapid destruction of the vineyards of France and the rest of Europe. Between 1870 and 1881 one and a half million acres of French vineyards were destroyed and between 1877 and 1889 wine production there fell 59%. It was a monumental disaster.

Not surprisingly American imports of French wine in bulk during these years collapsed, dropping 69% between 1873 and 1881, a decline of over four million gallons during the latter year alone. At the same time American duties on foreign wine were raised in 1874 and 1883 to an almost prohibitive level. The French reaction to their disaster was to search out ways to save their vineyards, but the immediate response of French wine merchants was to produce large amounts of adulterated and fabricated wine. This combination of events, along with the softening of the effects of the general depression in the United States, firmed California wine and grape prices in 1877. In 1878 they rose and continued to do so for several years.

California wine leaders were overjoyed. Professor Hilgard was happy to see that "things have assumed a very different aspect," even if "this change is due to the misfortunes of our neighbors." Arpad Haraszthy almost crowed: "France has laid the whole world under tribute for two hundred years for wine . . . ." Now California would supply France and the rest of the world. Historian Bancroft remarked that "A sound excitement set in . . . ." And there was no more excitement anywhere than in the Santa Clara Valley and the Santa Cruz Mountains.[1]

Westside, or today's Cupertino, was a sea of vines by the 1880's. This is an 1889 view of the foothills looking south from the roof of Captain Merithew's ranch over McClellan Road toward the Stelling ranch. *(Dunbar Collection)*

The five years from 1880 to 1885 transformed the region's winegrowing into a huge, complicated industry few of the early pioneers would have recognized. Growth was the order of the day and organization the guiding principle. This growth was on a scale never imagined. It followed a pattern that was repeated in many parts of the state and which opened up several new districts to winegrowing. It is not by chance that many of California's older wineries are celebrating centennials between 1979 and 1985. It is sad to note, however, that there is only one winery operation in this area still functioning today out of the scores founded here in these years. This is the Novitiate at Los Gatos.

CUPERTINO/WEST SIDE

The valley west of San Jose and Santa Clara and north of Saratoga up to Mountain View was called West Side in the early years and picked up the name Cupertino officially after the turn of the century. In the 1870's there was little intensive agriculture here, mostly huge ranches, large parts of which were totally undeveloped.

Viticulture had moved into the area when Elisha Stephens planted his little vineyard near the site of today's Blackberry Farm. Later the Jesuits built Villa Maria and planted their vineyards on the slopes of Stevens Creek Canyon. The other viticultural pioneers here were Samuel R. Williams, who planted his vineyard in 1870, and Norman Porter, who soon sold his development to Captain Joseph C. Merithew. Just to the north, near Mountain View, A.C. Hollenbeck and John Snyder had put out large vineyards in the late 70s. This "leafing out" of the district was followed by a far more luxuriant growth in the next decade.

A virtual storm of vine planting swept the West Side between 1880 and 1885. By the middle of the decade thousands of acres of vines had been planted and the country was transformed into a gigantic vineyard. Capitalists and local farmers all raced to buy land and take advantage of the rising grape prices. Those who owned land expanded their operations or were scorned for being overly conservative. There were few of these, and none by 1890.

San Francisco newspapermen filled the press with the attractions of the place. Wetmore and Haraszthy said that it was California's Medoc, the home of the greatest clarets to come. Part of its attraction was its position in the valley's thermal belt. The San Francisco *Bulletin* wrote that "Jack Frost seldom ventures, even when holding high carnival in San Jose." By 1887 that paper stated that "as far as the eye

Captain Merithew's home and "Prospect Vineyard" included fifty acres on McClellan Road, Cupertino, located on portions of today's De Anza College campus site. *(Dunbar Collection)*

48

can reach you will see thousands of acres of vines, stretching in places far up toward the summit of the Santa Cruz Mountains." It was quite an explosion and when the dust settled local folk realized that there weren't enough wineries to take care of all the grapes. By the end of the decade there were too many grapes, whatever the number of wineries.

J.B.J. Portal

The local man who did the most to promote the West Side boom was a Frenchman who came here in 1869 and made his money in San Jose real estate. "Louis" Portal, as his friends always called Jean Baptiste Jules, had bought a little piece of land west of town in 1872 and imported several varieties of Burgundy grapes, including the Black Burgundy and Ploussard. He moved out on Stevens Creek Road and in 1878 planted his new Burgundy Vineyard with 30 acres of good varieties. He expanded these plantings and built a very sizeable winery where he made some of the best red wine in the valley for over a decade.

Portal was an active leader of the valley's winemakers and vineyardists and did much to promote an emphasis on better quality grapes for better wine. He was a spirited man and could make enemies as easily as friends. He even became involved in a somewhat riotous libel suit in 1884 over a negative public statement made by another hot-headed Frenchman about his wines. Portal built a magnificent Victorian mansion on the street that still bears his name. It was one of Cupertino's finest landmarks until torn down in 1959.

He went back to France several times during these years, but in 1893 he went back to stay, having run off with his beautiful blond second cousin, abandoning his wife and seven children. Mathilde Portal continued to operate the Burgundy Vineyard until the late 1890s when debts and phylloxera forced her to sell. [2]

Joseph C. Merithew

An interesting fact of West Side demography was the settlement here between 1877 and 1888 of thirteen retired sea captains and their families. Many of them established vineyards and some had wineries. The most important was Joseph C. Merithew, who was to become the grand old man of Cupertino viticulture and a leader of a totally different sort than Portal, although both agreed on the importance of better varieties for better wine.

In 1879 Merithew bought Norman Porter's 1871 vineyard, just south of Stevens Creek Road, and named it Prospect Vineyard. He made his first wine in that year. Merithew was a leader from the beginning, stable, intelligent, honest and a true friend of the local wine industry, small as his 40 acre operation was. He was president of both the local and county viticultural societies and was a regular speaker at winegrowers' meetings in Northern California.

He made good table wines, particularly his Sylvaner, White Riesling and Zinfandel. But it was his sweet wine and brandy that usually won plaudits. He produced one of the few California sherries that tasted like sherry. This came from his careful vinification and from his ageing process. He had glass covered compartments in the ground where he baked his sherries in the sun to get a nutty, authentic flavor. At the Columbian Exposition in 1893 his sherry, port and brandy all won awards, the port receiving a particularly friendly evaluation from Charles Oldham, the English expert.

Merithew fought on through the hard times of the 1890s and continued to produce wines of high quality. He opened as small "Family Wine Store" in San Jose in 1897. In these years he even had some success shipping his better wines to England and to the East Coast. He was badly injured by a runaway at the age of 79 and died three years later in 1904, remembered by all who knew him as a good man who made very good wine.[3]

John T. Doyle

The most important single individual in the history of the West Side wine industry was John Thomas Doyle. In fact he gave Cupertino its name, after the little creek in the area. In the history of California and the West, Doyle's leadership in the world of wine would probably rate no more than a footnote in relationship to his eminent political position in the state and his great reputation as a trial lawyer and scholar. He first settled his family in 1866 on a great estate in Menlo Park where he planted a large Charbono vineyard. He was bitten by the winemaking bug and was one of the first to move into the West Side in 1880, purchasing a huge tract of land amounting to 320 acres near today's McClellan Road and Foothill Boulevard.

He had a huge vineyard planted and in 1880 tried to make wine from some poor grapes already growing there. He had them trod in a horse trough and the result was terrible. It was the last poor vintage for the Cupertino Wine Company. He built a winery and planted the very best varietals, even importing a large number from Europe. In 1883 he donated a two acre plot to the University of California to act as a viticultural experiment station. Here he and Professor Hilgard experimented with the usual premium varieties and with Doyle's imports, which included Nebbiolo, Barbera, Pinot St. George, Petite Sirah, Meunier, Refosco and Cabernet Franc. Some of his Italian imports were the first of the kind to arrive in California, his Barbera being particularly successful.[4]

By 1888 Doyle had 200 acres of grapes and had built a second winery near the first. He called it Las Palmas. The double row of Washington palms off Foothill Boulevard today marks the old entrance. This 1886 winery was a four story masterpiece, one of first truly modern, automated facilities in the state. Hilgard loved its "rational and careful" operation

Doyle was a leader and champion of the state's winemakers in their battle with the economic powers in San Francisco that controlled much of the wine industry. He could be a bitter foe of Charles Wetmore when the Commissioner seemed to truckle to these interests. Doyle served on the State Board of Viticultural Commissioners for three terms and was its president for one. He also led the campaign for the use of resistant rootstock in the war against phylloxera.

His wines from the Cupertino Wine Company were probably the best in the state, year in-year out, bottle for bottle, at least as far as large scale operations were concerned. His clarets, particularly his 1890 Cabernet Franc, were winners at the Columbian Exposition. At Bordeaux his wines won a silver medal in 1895, the only such award won by any California winery. The same year his clarets again triumphed, this time at the Berlin Exposition.

The 1906 earthquake shattered both of Doyle's wineries and he died later in the year at the age of 87. But by then he had retired and his interests were being handled by the California Wine Association, once his great enemy. His family sold off the vineyards to developers in 1912.[5]

There were numerous other important winery operations in the Cupertino area of the West Side. The Williams Union Winery at the Corner of Stelling and Stevens Creek Road was one of the largest. Richard Heney's Chateau Ricardo developed a great reputation for its estate bottled clarets. Charles Baldwin built a great estate on Stevens Creek Road and put in a large vineyard and a fine winery, the latter serving today as the book store at De Anza College and his home, the Petite Trianon, housing the California History Center. Down the road Alexander Montgomery, a fiery little Irishman, built a large winery and distillery and made a name for himself with his peach and prune brandies. He also made Kosher table wine, always having a Rabbi present when such products were being produced. Closer to Santa

Westside families are off on an outing in Richard Heney's "Chateau Ricardo" wine delivery truck. This extensive vineyard was on the south side of the 280-Foothill Expressway intersection, where once a pet cemetery, now condominiums stand.

Clara the S.P. Collins and the Pierce brothers' were large and important.

When the decade was over and the planting and winery building binge had subsided, there were over 4000 acres of vines on the West Side from Gubserville above Saratoga up to Mountain View. There were 39 wineries in the area and about 150 commercial wine growers, two thirds of whom had spreads of 15 acres or more. Where there had been grain and hay fields a decade before, there was now a sea of vines. [6]

MOUNTAIN VIEW AND NORTH

There was no dividing line between the Cupertino and Mountain View winegrowing districts. This sea of vines curved up around the foothills of the thermal belt in an almost solid mass.

The greatest winery operation in the Mountain View district, actually in the entire county, was that of Delphin M. Delmas, the son of Antoine Delmas. Like Doyle, Delmas was one of the most noted trial lawyers in the United States, and as an orator was said to have been more eloquent than William Jennings Bryan. He had graduated from Santa Clara College in 1862 at the age of 18 and from Yale law school three years later. At the age of 23 he was elected San Jose's district attorney. Delmas was attracted by the prospects of winegrowing. His father was still alive and the younger man certainly remembered the great days of Antoine's importance. In the early 1880s Delphin purchased several pieces of adjoining land along El Camino Real next to what is today the Cherry Chase Golf Course. He planted over 300 acres of wine grapes and built a huge winery in 1887 that eventually had a capacity of half a million gallons. For all its size, however, we do not hear any claims as to the high quality of the production at Casa Delmas. [7]

The best wine here was certainly made by C.P. Howe whose 190,000 gallon winery was just south of the Delmas estate. He won awards for his Riesling, Sauterne and Cabernet Sauvignon. Bernard Distal and John Bergin were the other important winegrowers in the area.

To the north around the little town of Mayfield, today a part of Palo Alto, there were several vineyards amounting to about 300 acres and a few small wineries. The most important was operated by A.P. Hotaling, the famous San Francisco liquor dealer, who also had a 60 acre vineyard there.

Just to the north was the most famous winegrower of them all, Leland Stanford. In 1876 he purchased George Gordon's Mayfield Grange property and proceeded to expand his holdings until the

"Farm" eventually amounted to over 10,000 acres. There had been a vineyard there and Stanford expanded it to 158 acres. In 1888 he built a brick winery that produced 60,000 gallons that year. His Palo Alto Vineyard wines were sold in the east for many years under the Stanford label. After his death in 1893, and after Palo Alto village had been established as a dry town, to protect students at the new University, Mrs. Jane Stanford ordered the manager of the winery to sell no more wine to local folks, particularly the students. The place soon ended its winemaking operations and in 1909 was converted into a student dormitory. In later years it served as a dairy barn, and today still stands on the Stanford grounds, functioning as a commercial complex. [8]

MONTEBELLO RIDGE

Standing in the foothills of Cupertino or Mountain View one looks up to a high ridge to the west of the valley, over 2,000 feet in height. It is Montebello, the center piece of the great *Chaine d'Or*, or golden chain of highland wine country, which today produces some of the greatest wines in America. To look up was to see a sylvan wilderness in 1880. By 1890 it was a well established wine district.

The Villa Maria had begun planting vineyards at the bottom of the Ridge in the 1870s. Their foreman had arrived here from Italy in 1872 and, encouraged by the fathers, Vincent Picchetti bought 160 acres above the Villa in 1877 and planted grape vines and fruit trees. In 1896 he built a fine little winery that still stands on the property, now part of a regional park.

Picchetti was soon followed by other growers: Coreless, Roffo, Bellomi, Fisher, Zabeldano. More important, he was also followed by others interested in winemaking, but with a rather more idealistic attitude toward quality. To the top of the Ridge in 1886 came San Francisco physician Osea Perrone, who bought 180 acres there indirectly from Enrico Bressi, who had homesteaded the place the year before. Perrone established his Montebello Vineyards and built a great winery and summer home, as well as a fairly lucrative wine business. [9]

The greatest of the first generation Montebello winemakers was Pierre Klein, an Alsatian who came to California in 1875. Four years later he opened the Occidental Restaurant in San Francisco. Eventually in 1888 his skills and reputation placed the management of the restaurant and tasting room of the State Board of Viticultural Commissioners in his hands.

Klein had become an ardent advocate of California wine at its best and was appalled at some of the cheap stuff that often carried the state's name to the drinking public. He was particularly disgusted by the amount of fairly good California wine that had to pass under phony French labels to be accepted by this country's wine drinkers. Thus, he emphasized good California wine at his restaurant and was the perfect man for Wetmore to select as his manager.

Also in 1888 Klein purchased 160 acres about halfway up Montebello Ridge and gradually developed one of the finest wine establishments in the state. He planted Mira Valle to the vines of Bordeaux's Medoc: Cabernet Sauvignon, Merlot, Cabernet Franc and Petite Verdot. He established his own brand, selling only in glass, and sold mostly to other good restaurants. His approach to viticulture and winemaking was impeccable. Every unripe bunch was removed before it reached the fermenting tank. "I never minded the expense," he wrote, "as I wanted to make a thorough test and satisfy my ambition."

In 1895 Klein was persuaded to enter his wine in the Bordeaux Exposition, where he took an honorable mention for an 1891 vintage in which he took little pride. The next year he won medals at Atlanta and Brussels. The success of his Mira Valle Cabernets reached its zenith in 1900 when he won the gold medal at the Paris Exposition. From then on his wine, and that of Emmett Rixford in Woodside, gave the *Chaine d'Or* clarets of the Santa Cruz Mountains a reputation for excellence that carried through Prohibition and down to the present time. Klein continued his great work until 1910 when he retired, selling off his place in 1913. He settled in Mountain View where, in poor health and grieved by his wife's death, he committed suicide in 1922. Pierre Klein's name is much revered by the winemakers of the *Chaine d'Or* today. [10]

WOODSIDE-PORTOLA VALLEY

The head of the *Chaine d'Or* is a hilly country around Woodside in San Mateo County. The wine boom hit this area of the Santa Cruz Mountains even more forcefully than at Montebello. By 1890 there were about 800 acres of wine grapes growing in the area, almost all of them planted in the previous decade. There were seven wineries now to handle the vintage, some of them fairly large. San Francisco attorney Edgar F. Preston had the most impressive operation with 80 acres of vines, an 1887 winery with a capacity of 175,00 gallons and a beautiful home on Old La Honda Road, owned by the Schilling family after 1912. One reporter in 1891 stated that Preston had made the best three year old claret available then. Nearby S.L. Jones's Hazelwood Farm

California's display at the Exposition of the Societé Philomathique, Bordeaux, France. Pierre Klein's winery located on Montebello Road, Cupertino (where the Jimsomare-Schwabacher ranch is today) won a silver medal for its Cabernet at this Exposition.

Ricordando momenti indimenticabili ospiti dai Sig. Picchetti. Offr. O.Adami 45…

The Italian community actively contributed to the development of Westside viticulture. Vincenso Picchetti (standing front and center of car with flags) tended vines at the Jesuit retreat, Villa Maria. He was the first person to open up the Montebello area to grape growing. His home, shown above, is now part of the Midpeninsula Regional Park District. (*Picchetti Collection*) had 85 acres in vines and made 60,000 gallons in 1890. [11]

The best of them was one of the smallest, the vineyard and winery of Emmett H. Rixford. He called his place La Questa, a 40 acre plot he purchased in 1883 above today's town of Woodside. It had a little hogback ridge, what the Spanish call a *cuesta*, the spot still easily seen from Interstate 280, west of the Woodside turnoff.

Rixford was certainly the most scholarly of all California's practical winemakers before the twentieth century. In 1887, he published *The Wine Press and the Cellar*, a meticulous compilation of the best winemaking practices then known. He planted La Questa to red Bordeaux wine varieties, in the precise proportion as they were then grown at Chateau Margaux, whose wine he dearly loved.

By the turn of the century Rixford's reputation was remarkable. He stood with Pierre Klein and Napa's Tiburcio Parrott as a master of California wine in the Medoc style. His wine was hailed on both sides of the Atlantic. It was even the favorite of the anti-California publisher of the eastern *American Wine Press*. The estate bottled La Questa Cabernet won a string of awards, topped by a gold medal at the Panama-Pacific Exposition in 1915. Rixford lived until 1928, selling his grapes to home winemakers during the dry years. His old vines still live and produce wine grapes. [12]

SARATOGA/LOS GATOS

The boom in winegrowing of the 1880s struck the West Side south of the Cupertino area, but not nearly so intensely as it had to the north. Nevertheless, the land around Saratoga and Los Gatos did become important vineyard country as did the hills behind the towns. There was one fairly important area, north of Saratoga, then called the Lincoln district, for the school there. The Lincoln Winery stood at the crossroads of Prospect and Saratoga-Sunnyvale Roads and was run by Peter Ball in conjunction with partners that included the owners of F. Brassy & Co., San Jose's leading liquor merchants at the turn of the century. Ball made some of the best Zinfandel claret on the West Side. The winery, which burned down in 1902, was the first in the area to use electricity. To the west on Prospect were the John Bubb and Henry Farr wineries, and H.W. Hollenbeck's Buckhorn Winery. [13]

William Pfeffer

As noted in other places in this study, the most significant operation is not always among the largest. So it was in the Lincoln district. In 1869 William Pfeffer had settled here from Illinois, having first worked in the Yount vineyard in Napa Valley. On this 160 acres above Prospect Road he ran a thoroughly diversified agricultural establishment, but his great love was experimental viticulture and winemaking. He had a 17 acre vineyard planted to contours, one acre of which he laid aside for his experiments. He also had an elegant little winery whose 1883 Cabernet Sauvignon moved Charles Wetmore to claim it the most like that of the Medoc he had ever tasted from California

Pfeffer was a fanatic for quality in wine and did not believe that really great wine could be made at large wineries. He argued that every vineyardist with premium varietals should be his own winemaker. In this he was about a century ahead of his time, when hundreds of winegrowers in the 1970s would dot Northern California with their "boutique" wineries.

It was in the area of grape breeding that he made his greatest contribution to California wine. He was in the forefront in the work that sought the proper American resistant rootstock as defense against the phylloxera. He was a friend of Thomas V. Munson, the great Texas grape breeder, and over the years worked closely with George Husmann and others. He wrote regularly on the topic in a number of publications and distinguised himself by long resisting the notion that the Rupestris St. George was a universal rootstock for California, even though it had become accepted as such for over half a century.

Pfeffer also bred and developed wine grape vines, although few ever caught on among growers. One did have a fairly good following, appropriately named Pfeffer Cabernet. It was a controversial grape and was not planted after Prohibition. There is one good plot still standing in Almaden's Cienega Vineyard in San Benito County, planted shortly after the turn of the century. The vines still produce exceptionally fine claret wine, quite tasty and, appropriately, quite peppery.

After his death in 1910 Pfeffer's estate was sold by the family to Fremont Older, the famed San Francisco newspaper editor. He and his wife were little interested in agriculture and Pfeffer's land was allowed to return to nature. Today one would need a machete to pass through what once had been one of the finest little vineyards in California.[14]

The vineyard planting craze was quite feverish around the towns of Los Gatos and Saratoga in these years. To the normal frenzy was added the fact that in 1877 the railroad had arrived in Los Gatos and within three years the South Pacific Coast railroad had literally punched its way through the mountains to Santa Cruz and was now serving the area between. By the end of the decade there were over 2,000 acres of wine grapes planted by people who picked up their mail in these two towns, and there were 18 wineries. The vineyard spreads around Saratoga tended to be much larger in size than those in the Los Gatos area.

But with this planting did not come the immediate building of wineries. This became something of a problem when the flood of grapes from vines coming into production caused prices to soften. As a result two gigantic establishments were build on a sort of corporate cooperative principle.

In 1885 the Los Gatos-Saratoga Winery was founded and built in time for the vintage at Austin Corners, between the two towns. By 1889 the huge wooden winery was making 120,000 gallons and by 1900 was up to 350,000. Under the supervision of three outstanding managers the winery built up a really excellent reputation for its whites and clarets and had a good trade in England. When Prohibition came the huge place was knocked down and the lumber sold to ranchers in the area. [15]

Even more important to the prosperity of local growers was the building of the Los Gatos Cooperative Winery in 1886. It was a huge multi-story affair which stood against the hill behind where the Town Library is today. By 1889 the Co-op was making over 300,000 gallons of wine and by the end of the 1890s was the county's largest producer. It served as a very necessary "home" for local growers' grapes and eventually became an important part of the California Wine Association. Many of the grapes made up at the Co-op came down from the Santa Cruz Mountains. In fact, the winery's manager for years, William B. Rankin, was himself an important mountain winegrower with a large estate near Glenwood. [16]

NEW ALMADEN — LEFRANC/MASSON

When Charles Le Franc was killed in 1887 trying to stop a runaway, the continuity of New Almaden history was sharply untracked. The estate, which included the Lefranc building downtown, went to Charles's three children, Henry, Louise and Marie. Meanwhile another person had arrived on the scene, a young Burgundian named Paul Masson, who had first come to California in 1878. He met Lefranc, visited New Almaden and took some business courses at San Jose's University of the Pacific. Masson had gone back to France in

60

1880 but was encouraged to return to California by the ugly effects of the phylloxera in Burgundy. Masson went to work for Lefranc and became very much involved with the overall business of the winery.

Very soon after Charles's death Masson married Louise and set off for France on an extended honeymoon. While there he looked into the purchase of French Champagne making equipment and on his return formed a partnership, Lefranc & Masson, with brother-in-law Henry. It is clear that part of the purpose of the partnership was to produce a proper sparkling wine in the style and with the methods of Champagne. This arrangement did not in any way affect the ownership of New Almaden or other Lefranc properties, which remained in the hands of the three children.

Masson's job was also to market New Almaden products. He also started up a wholesale retail and liquor business on his own. The Lefranc wines continued to appear under the New Almaden label. By 1891 Masson's experiments on a bottle fermented Champagne were in full swing, with the help of an imported Champagne expert and good French equipment. In May of 1892 Masson released his first Champagne and in September the partnership with Henry was terminated. He acquired needed capital to continue on his own but kept his operation in the basement of the Lefranc building. Later he transfered his cellars to the basement of San Jose's Vendome Hotel. Here a visitor remarked that, although Mr. Masson thought his operation a nice little place, it was "in reality, a very nice, large place."

Masson used New Almaden wine to produce his Champagne, but was not satisfied with the quality of the grapes grown on the valley floor. He needed a cooler area and he needed better Champagne grape varieties. He apparently maintained fairly cordial business relations with Henry Lefranc, although on one occasion Henry took public umbrage in the press for Masson's tendency to portray himself as the sole source of energy in the family's businesses.

In 1896 Masson found a piece of land that suited his needs, above Pierce Road in the Mt. Eden district of Saratoga. As the Saratoga *Item* put it on November 20, "Paul Masson of San Jose was up yesterday to look over his property interests . . . ." He had purchased the foreclosed property of Alexander Rodoni, who had gone bankrupt after backing an unsuccessful teamster company. Rodoni had a 12 acre vineyard and a small winemaking facility. In the next years Masson imported and planted better varieties and set about establishing himself as America's premier champagne producer. [15]

Map and extracts from the 1885 *Santa Clara Valley Agricultural and Viticultural Newspa*

OUR COUNTY
No. 6.

THE CUPERTINO DISTRICT—THE GREAT GRAPE-GROWING SECTION—THE BORDEAUX OF THE PACIFIC COAST.

The accompany maps includes the district Westward from the Saratoga and Mountain View road, and North from the road leading to Mill's Spring.

SARATOGA AND MOUNTAIN VIEW ROAD.

J. E. ABBOTT.—46 54-100 acres; 10 acres French prunes, and about 100 trees of assorted varieties planted last Winter; the remainder grain land.

D. E. ROOT, "Magnolia Villa."—40 acres; 15,000 vines 2 years old, of which 7,000 are Charbono, 3,500 Mataro, 3,500 Zinfandel, and 1 acre Golden Chasselas, and other table varieties; 13 acres French prunes, and family orchard of 80 trees, 2 years old, raspberries and blackberries.

B. W. HOLLENBECK, "Lone Oak Ranch." 120 acres; 45 of which are in orchard and vineyard; of trees there are 100 apples, 300 prunes, and an assortment of cherries, plums, peaches and pears, from 1 to 3 years old; 20 acres of vines are 3 years old and 10 acres 2 years old; the varieties are Zinfandel, Mataro, Charbono, Trousseau and a few Muscat; remainder of the place grain and pasture.

E. VAN DINE.—45 acres; 10 acres French prunes, and an assorted family orchard recently planted; 20 acres in vines, all Zinfandel and Mataro, except 1 acre each of Muscat and Flame Tokay, 2 years old.

C. W. PROCTOR.—36 acres; 31 of which are in orchard; 1,600 French prunes, 130 apples, Newtown Pippins, Jonathan and Bellflower; 150 Bartlett pears, 35 plums, 175 peaches, 200 Moorpark apricots, 50 cherries, and 40 orange quince.

D. FREEMAN.—40 acres. Mr. Freeman resides in Santa Clara, and there was no one on the place when we called. There are a very few trees and about 28 acres of vines, 2 years old, of Zinfandel, Mataro, Grenache and Muscat.

W. GINTY.—25 acres; 14 acres French prunes, 100 trees of family orchard, and the remainder peaches and apples, alternately, with a view of retaining the more profitable variety when it becomes necessary to remove a portion; trees now 3 years old. 40 acres about a mile further north, planted last Winter; one-half in vineyard and one-half in pear, apricot, and cherry trees.

GASSETT AND MORGAN.—25 acres; 500 apricots, 200 pears, 100 peaches, 100 of assorted varieties, 50 cherries and 15 acres of French prunes, 3 years old; 3 acres of grapes.

J. B. WING.—55 acres; all French prunes 1 and 2 years old.

F. M. JOLLYMAN.—32 acres; all planted; 16 acres are in Muscat grapes, 1 and 2 years old, and 16 acres in trees, 500 of which are prunes, 500 almonds, 300 pears, and the remainder peaches, cherries, apples and plums 2 and 3 years old.

T. KERWIN.—98 acres; about 1 acre of family orchard and 60 acres in vines 4 years old; varieties are Charbono, Zinfandel, Trousseau, Mataro, Cabernet, Malbec, Carignan, Grenache, Black Pinot, Golden Chasselas and Muscat; remainder of place in grain.

PRESBYTERIAN CHURCH.—1 acre; and a neat little place of worship.

D. DURKEE.—30 acres; found no one on the place; from the best information we learn he has 10 acres in vines, mostly Muscat, and 20 acres in peach, prune and apricot trees, 1 and 2 years old.

BUBB ROAD.

R. C. STILLER.—40 acres; 15 acres of grapes 2/3 4 years old, and 1/3 1 years old; Zinfandel, Malbec, Cabernet, Reissling and Charbono; 4 acres prunes, 7 acres pears, 4 acres apricots, 5 acres apples and a few peaches, 4 years old.

A. REGNART.—40 acres; all in grain, owner now in England.

J. P. BUBB.—276 acres; 25 or 30 acres of fruit trees and 7 acres nuts; 8 acres are prunes, and the remainder in other varieties; 22 acres of grapes, some are Mission at least 30 years old, and giving very heavy crops, the remainder Mataro, Charbono and Cabernet. There are about 200 old fruit trees, 25 to 30 years old, among which are peach trees still growing excellent fruit; remainder of place devoted to hay, grain and stock.

HENRY FARR.—343 acres; family orchard of about 400 trees consisting of nectarines, plums, peaches, apricots, pears, cherries, prunes, and almonds; about 50 acres of grapes 2, 3 and 4 years old, of which 1½ acres are Mission and the rest Malvoisie, Charbono, Trousseau, and Mataro, with 4 acres Cabernet and some Reissling and Muscat recently planted.

CAPT. J. BERNARD.—80 acres; was not at home when we called; should say he has about 40 acres in cultivation, 8 to 10 acres of vineyard and 6 to 8 of orchard, planted in peaches, apricots, prunes, and almonds.

WM. PFEFFER.—160 acres; orchard of 10 or more acres, containing 200 apricot, 50 apple, 150 pear, 70 peach, 500 prune, and 230 almond trees all in bearing; vineyard of 10 acres or more of vines from 5 to 16 years old; there 3 acres Cabernet Franc, 1 acre Muscat, 1½ Zinfandel, ½ Reissling, and the remainder Mataro, Carignan, Grenache, Trousseau, Cabernet Sauvignan, Malbec and Seedless Sultana; has made raisins of the latter variety for 4 or 5 years, and a good white wine; makes his grape crop into wine at his own winery.

N. HAYNES.—19 acres; owner not at home when we called; place seems about three-fourths planted in orchard and vineyard.

J. J. WALKER.—20 acres; 200 apples, 200 pears, 150 peaches, and 15 acres of French prunes.

LOUISE C. SPANGENBERG.—66 acres; 5 acres silver prunes and cherries, planted last year; 9 apricots, 2 cherries, 6 pears, several varieties of prunes, plums and peaches; 6 acres of grapes planted last year, Mataro, Trousseau and Riparia for grafting.

J. D. WILLIAMS.—20 acres; the vineyard occupies about 19 acres, is 2 years old, and the varieties are Zinfandel, Mataro, Charbono and Trousseau; small family orchard.

H. B. CHAMPION.—Two parcels, one of 20, and one of 15 acres; on the 20 acres are 1,984 prune trees, 500 peaches, and 96 apricots; on the 15 acres are 100 cherries, 200 egg plums, 108 prunes, 111 silver prunes, 22 apricots, 280 apples, in 3 or 4 varieties, 300 pears, 525 peaches, and 10 trees of assorted kinds.

MRS. E. L. WATSON.—25 acres; 2,000 French prunes, 60 silver prunes, 112 cherries, 182 egg plums, 130 pears, 98 apricots, 24 peaches, and a number of miscellaneous trees of English walnut, quince, almond, etc.

E. HANRAHAN.—141 acres; mostly in grain, only a few trees and vines about the house.

H. REGNART.—40 acres; vineyard of 24 acres 3 years old, Zinfandel, Mataro and Charbono; 500 prune and 225 peach trees, and a family orchard, part of it in old trees.

JOHN STELLING.—160 acres; 40 acres are in vines, and 40 in vines and trees planted together; the first 40 are in Zinfandel, Charbono, Trousseau and Cabernet, and the second 40 is Charbono, Zinfandel and Muscat, 3 years old; the trees are ½ almonds and German and French prunes, and a few of an assortment, 3,000 almonds in all; 10 acres cut off by creek channel, all in fruit, prunes, egg plums, and family orchard.

MRS. A. MEUNIER.—80 acres; about 20,-000 vines planted 2 and 3 years old; 2 year-old vines are Zinfandel, Charbono and Mataro, and the other Grenache, Petit Pinot, White Pinot, Cabernet, Carignan and Portal Ploussard; there are 70 prune, 70 apricot, and an assortment of apple, peach, pear, plum and cherry trees. Reached by road through Hanrahan's.

A. SOMERVILLE.—80 acres; family orchard of about 2 acres and a vineyard of several acres all in table grapes.

WM. ETCHELL, Vallejo.—40 acres; 24,-000 vines 2 and 3 years old, of Petit Pinot, Zinfandel, Mataro, Charbono, Carignan, Grenache and Sauvignon; 3 acres French prunes, 3 years old and an acre of assorted varieties for family orchard one year old.

REGNART'S ROAD.

A private road recently laid out leaves the Bubb road south of Hanrahan's and leads into the hills.

J. F. MALLATRATT.—4 acres; mostly all silver prunes, with a few apricots and peaches 2 years old.

THEO. SCHARFF.—29 70-100 acres in two parcels; one reached from the Bubb road and the other by Regnart's. On the 10 acre piece are 6 acres Oregon Silver prunes and French prunes, and 4 acres grapes, Mataro and Zinfandel; of the 19 acre piece 15 acres were planted last spring in Mataro, Zinfandel, Grenache, Charbono, Trousseau and Chasselas.

W. REGNART.—80 acres; 9,000 vines 1 and 2 years old, Zinfandel, Mataro, Golden Chasselas, Petit Pinot, Sweetwater and Charbono; 1,500 trees, 900 of which are prunes, 200 apricots, and the remainder an assortment of various kinds, 1 and 2 years old; this ranch is a sample of what may be made from the rough mountain lands.

R. REGNART.—Has 40 acres adjoining; on which 9,000 Charbono vines, and 700 prune trees were planted last year.

MARKHAM.—160 acres; 10 or 12 acres newly planted in trees and vines.

MANN.—160 acres; several acres planted last spring, both of trees and vines.

THE STELLING ROAD.

Leads west from the Mountain View road to Cupertino.

J. B. WING AND A. M. BARKER.—40 acres; all in vines planted last spring; 30 acres are Mataro and 10 are Grenache.

CAPT. A. H. WOOD AND J. B. LUTHER. 40 acres; 25 acres are planted in vines now 4 years old; the varieties are Charbono, Mataro, Black Malvoisie and Muscat; there are 5 acres peaches and 10 acres cherries, and other fruits one year old.

CAPT. J. C. MERITHEW, "Prospect Vineyard."—50 acres; 10 acres walnuts, almonds, and prunes, 11 years old, and 40 acres of vines of same age; there are 10 acres Trousseau, 10 acres Charbono, 8 of Black Prince, 3 of Grenache, and the remainder Muscat and other sorts; counting back for 5 years this vineyard has given an average of 5 tons per acre; almonds average $75 per acre for same time; walnut trees have borne only lightly till this year; makes up his own grapes into wine and has a distillery for brandy of which he produced 700 gallons last year. He is building a fine large cistern for rain water which would seem a good plan for others to follow.

DR. W. F. GUNKEL, "Bonnie View."—36 acres; a vineyard of 3 acres Malbec vines 12 acres of almonds 5 years old, 3 acres silver prunes, and the remainder French prunes.

G. J. BYRNE, "Glen Brook."—55 acres; a small orchard planted some years ago and a few acres of vineyard, Mission grapes.

J. T. DOYLE.—Has 380 acres in four parcels of 20, 50, 150 and 160 acres; of the 160 acre piece 56 acres are in prunes. The 150 acre parcel is known as "Palmas," taking its name from a double row of palm trees along the principal avenue; of this, 140 acres are in vines, 7 acres in prunes, and 3 acres waste land along the creek. The vineyard is divided into blocks as shown on our map; approportionately there are 60 acres Charbono, 3½ each of Trousseau and Malbec, 1½ of Reissling, 1¾ Mataro, 40 acres Cabernet, and two blocks or about 3½ acres have been given to the University of California for experimental purposes and are now planted in over 40 varieties. The 50 acre vineyard is divided into 32 blocks all of which are Charbono, except 3 blocks of Zinfandel and 2 of Cabernet. The 20 acre parcel has 10 acres of Grenache and Carignan, the remainder occupied by wine house and cellars and other purposes. Mr. Doyle makes his own wine and has a large winery on each side of the creek, that on the west side being connected with his extensive cellars by a pipe for the convenient transfer of wines. Some statements of the yield of these vineyards will be found on another page.

JOS. MCCLELLAN.—40 acres; on the south side of the road are 22 acres of Muscat and Tokay grapes, 200 prunes and 250 apricots; on the north side 4 acres pears, 3 of apricots, 1 of apples and peaches, 1 acre of nursery, and 1 acre of garden and pasture.

L. SELLENGER.—About 154 acres. We were unable to see Mr. Sellenger, and his foreman was unable to give us much information about the place. There is a fine residence and more than half of the place is set in vineyard and orchard in very fine cultivation.

ROAD UP STEVENS CREEK.

SANTA CLARA COLLEGE.—The Fathers of Santa Clara College have 310 acres purchased to provide a place of recreation and retirement during Summer vacation. It is nicely laid out in roads and pleasant walks; a pretty villa has been erected, a small chapel and several shrines on prominent points. Forty-six acres are in vineyard, partly Mission grapes, and the later planting are of the very

THE HILLS BEHIND

The tiny beginnings of viticulture in the Santa Cruz Mountains behind Los Gatos and Saratoga were greatly expanded during the 1880s. In the Mt. Eden area above Saratoga a few small vineyards were planted. These growers usually sold to Edward H. Guppy, who planted his El Monte Vineyard and built his winery on Mt. Eden Road in the mid 1880s.

In the hills along the Congress Springs Road a host of small family vineyards and little wineries were established in this period. Most of the families were Italian, French or Italian-Swiss, for whom viticulture and winemaking were but a part of a more complicated, diverse agricultural life, devoted mostly to raising fruit. A large number of these families were French, a remarkable percentage coming from a rural area in southeast France in the Department of Hautes Alpes, near the town of Gap. The names gave the area a distinct Gallic flavor: Reynaud, Rispaud, Ladarre, Bonnet, Estrade, Pourroy..

Behind Los Gatos, around Lexington, Alma and Glenwood, the pioneer winegrowers were able to sell off undeveloped land to newcomers in the 1880s and expand their own operations. Many of the names found on new deeds for land near the summit had a Germanic ring, for a German colony was developing on the slopes of Loma Prieta on land purchased from Ernst Emil Meyer, an 1881 settler, later known for his Mare Vista Winery nearby. By 1890 no less than 76 persons engaged in viticulture listed their mailing address as Wrights, Alma, Patchen or Glenwood, on the Santa Clara County side of the Santa Cruz Mountains. There were eleven small wineries with about 350 acres of wine grapes on the Santa Clara side, in addition to a flourishing table grape industry. When the table grape market went bad, any grapes that wouldn't sell would go into the fermenters at these small wineries.[16]

The Novitiate

Certainly the 1880s' most important and long lasting new wine establishment in the hills above the Santa Clara Valley was the Novitiate Winery. In fact, the winery of the Sacred Heart Novitiate of Los Gatos is today the oldest continuously operating winery in any of the three counties included in this study. The Jesuits chose the hills behind Los Gatos to establish a center for training novices and in 1886 took possession of Harvey Wilcox's 40 acres, already planted to orchards and a small vineyard of about four acres. The economic purpose of this purchase had been to acquire the land as an investment

Front of the Novitiate gravity flow winery. A good example of 19th century winery construction. One can see the top floor, the back of which received grapes for crushing, after which the juices would flow into the second floor fermenters, then down to the bottom floor for aging and storing. *(Novitiate Collection)*

The top floor of Novitiate winery where boxes full of grapes were dumped and crushed.

in diversified farming, but in the years to come the wine operations became dominant in the activities here.

The first vintage was in 1888 when Father Masnata bought some picking boxes and a small press from William Rankin. They made a few hundred gallons and made their first sale of sacramental wine to San Francisco's St. Ignatius College the next year. At first the winery was a wooden frame building, but in 1892 it was decided to pursue the wine business in earnest and plans were made to construct a large, concrete winery the next year since wine revenue had reached almost $2500.

The Jesuits expanded their land holdings over the years until the Novitiate's properties amounted to 460 acres. The wine business was a profitable one, helped considerably by the ready supply of vineyard and cellar workers available in the persons of the novices. The difference between life in these vineyards and in the rest of the industry can be inferred from an 1889 order to the novices that "hereafter until further orders, the novices will *work* in the vineyard for one hour before breakfast, instead of reading a history book in it."

By the mid 1890s the Novitiate was producing a very large number of table and dessert wines from many grape varieties, some of which had been brought from France by the first winemaker, Brother Jean Louis Olivier. They included Pinot Blanc, Cabernet, Mataro and Grenache, along with other varieties more commonly found in the valley.[17]

Vine Hill and Ben Lomond

The Vine Hill district in the hills above Santa Cruz is today one of the premier wine producing areas of California. In the period prior to Prohibition the area was much more vast than today. It began about four miles from the coast and ran inland five miles more, going from an elevation of about 400 feet up to about 1300 near Glenwood. By 1886 there were about 300 acres of vines in this area, the total growing to over 500 by the 1890s.

The Jarvis operations continued to grow and prosper during the years of the Wine Boom. John Jarvis combined with others to form the Santa Cruz Mountain Wine Company. A good sized winery was built along Branciforte Creek and large cellars were tunnelled into the cliffs there, the three totaling 380 feet in length. By the 1890s the winery had a capacity of 200,000 gallons and controlled about 60 acres of vineyard. The company was plagued by terrible fires throughout these years, but had an excellent business and fine reputation for its white wines and its Glenwood Zinfandel. John Jarvis' mountain grapes were also important in the production of the famous Jarvis Brandy in San Jose.[18]

In these days Jarvis did not have quite the quality reputation of some of his neighbors. Chief among these was George Bram, who probably made the best white wines in the mountains during these years. He had a 20,000 gallon operation and specialized in White Riesling and Semillon. Farther up the mountain was Henry Mel whose Fontenoy Vineyard produced a remarkable number of varietals. Hilgard was particularly impressed by Mel's Meunier and Chauche Noir in 1887.[19]

The master of red wine production lived near Scott's Valley, Dr. John A. Stewart, a tough Scotsman, whose Etta Hill Vineyard produced the best Cabernet in the mountains. He planted his vines at 2,000 to the acre and pruned them closely on cordons. He was the William Pfeffer of the Santa Cruz Mountains, the area's conscience concerning quality and grape varieties. He presented learned papers regularly and filled the Bay Area press with his views that singlemindedly flew in the face of the quality levellers who controlled much of the state's industry in the 1890s. He made about 15,000 gallons per year from his 60 acre vineyard, some of it white as well as red. Charles Oldham was impressed by his white Burgundy at Chicago in 1893, which may have been made from Chardonnay grapes. Stewart would have been happy to see today's prices for Cabernet Sauvignon grapes in comparison to those for ordinary grapes. During his life time his main complaint was the cheapness of fine wine grapes.[20]

Across the hills to the west another important wine district had developed by the 1880s in the Ben Lomond-Bonny Doon-Boulder Creek area. The main operation was the large Ben Lomond Wine Company, founded in 1886 by F.W. Billings of Redwood City and his son-in-law, J.F. Coope, who acted as manager until his death in 1902. The winery developed quite a reputation for its Grey Riesling, by far the predominant variety in their 90 acre vineyard. When Frona Wait wrote her famous book on California wine in 1889 she paid special attention to the company's white wine and predicted that the area would become "a future Chablis district" as the result of the Ben Lomond Grey Riesling, which had, she said, "the thin, delicate, flinty dryness of a true Chablis." Surprising as such a description seems when the ordinary quality of this grape is taken into consideration, the wine must have been fairly good, for it won many awards through the 1890s, capped by an honorable mention at the 1900 Paris Exposition.[21]

EVERGREEN

On the east side of the Santa Clara Valley the pioneer work begun by Pierre Pellier in the 1860s was followed in the 1880s by a great flood of commercial planting. Pellier had been joined in Evergreen by A.J. Fowler and H.L. Stevens in the 1870s, and had brought his own vineyard up to 80 acres by the end of the 1880s. Between 1883 and 1886 at least 1000 acres of wine grapes were planted in the Evergreen district. Of particular importance was the Yerba Buena Vineyard of 80 acres set out by the Paul O. Burns Company. This wine operation centered in downtown San Jose and is symbolic of the growing industrial character of the local wine industry during these years. Of even more importance in the long run was the establishment begun in 1889 in Evergreen by William Wehner. In the spring of that year his work force had begun planting vines on the 750 acre expanse of land he had purchased. A good part of this planting was on resistant rootsock. Soon there would be a good sized winery on the property.

The viticultural development of the southern portion of the Santa Clara Valley did not take place until after the 1880s. There were usually vineyards on the larger ranches, but these were rarely any real part of their economic life. In the valley itself, below Coyote, a large part of the land was still held in very large tracts that were not divided and sold until the turn of the century. Charles M. Weber still owned a large vineyard near Coyote and J.W. Ransome had a winery and large vineyard near Madrone. Farther south above Gilroy the O'Toole Winery and vineyard stood on gravelly soil.

The most important winegrowing took place in the hills to the west of the valley. Florin Cuzzard made wine from 30 acres below the Almaden Valley. In the Uvas area itself, and west of Gilroy near today's Hecker Pass Road, there were several small growers and a few winemakers, like Charles Francois at his 30 acre Uvas Vineyard. The wine industry really came to the area in 1889 when E.A. and Jonathon Hague, English brothers, bought a 360 acre portion of the old Solis Rancho and planted about 100 acres of wine grapes, founding the Solis Wine and Fruit Company, which dominated winegrowing in the area for years.[22]

In the city of San Jose the Wine Boom could best be seen in the establishment of several large industrial operations. The largest and least successful was the Paul O. Burns Wine Co., incorporated in 1886 with large vineyards in the Evergreen area. One of the stockholders was "Mountain Charley" McKiernan. The company owned an entire

Wine display at the 1893 Mid-Winter Fair, San Francisco. Note Captain Merithew's Prospect Vineyard, and Paul Burn's display, (lower right). Burn's plant took up an entire block in downtown San Jose in the 1890's. (*Dunbar Collection*)

city block bounded by 7th and San Salvador Streets. It was mainly a sweet wine and brandy factory with huge brandy stills that could produce thousands of gallons per day. The company made a great show of the operations, bottling some wine in glass with wire hoods. They had depots in the east, made shipments to Europe and had a thorough public relations campaign. By 1892 Burns was ousted as manager and arrested for embezzlement. By 1895 the company was in the process of dissolution.

More successful was the Pacific Winery, built in 1888 near the railroad, with about the same function as the Burns company. (McKiernan was also a stockholder here.) It bought up huge amounts of ordinary grapes and made equally ordinary wine and brandy, 400,000 gallons of wine in 1890. This company was far better managed and was purchased by Napa's Charles Carpy in 1891. Later it became a part of the California Wine Association.[23]

George Jarvis's wine and brandy works on River Street were the most successful. The key was good wine, excellent brandy and operations run by people with a solid connection to viticulture and a strong commitment to good wine. Jarvis's "Reisling" Brandy was a rival of General Naglee's, and his Glenwood Zinfandel was one of the best clarets in the state[23]

A reflective glance at the Wine Boom and the men who took part in this remarkable expansion may be useful in helping us understand the variables that faced the state's wine industry then and in later years, particularly in the years of the second Wine Boom from 1965 to 1980.

It is obvious that a large number of those involved in the 1880s were simply established farmers who saw wine grapes as another profitable crop. Some who could built wooden barns and called them wineries. They would be quite ready to turn to other crops when wine grapes became unprofitable.

Others were established winemen from the early days whose families had grown up on the land and who understood winegrowing as something more than a business. They passed on their vocation and their interest to their sons and daughters and helped give the wine interest needed continuity. Charles Lefranc and Pierre Pellier were such men.

Another group was made up of capitalist dilettantes who had made their fortunes elsewhere and who, in the 1880s, turned to the soil to devote themselves to a pastime to which they had a strong intellectual

71

Captain Joseph Merithew at the head of the table celebrates Thanksgiving dinner with some good wine, the Captain Dunbar family and Doctor Durgin. Merithew was a leading Westside vineyardist, highly respected for his production of sweet wines, especially a sherry he baked in bottles outdoors. *(Dunbar Collection)*

Joseph D. Williams home and large winery on the south side of Stevens Creek Boulevard and Stelling Road, Cupertino. An aggressive viticulturist, Williams was processing 160,000 - 200,000 gallons of wine a year by 1895. His home sat on a 14' high aging cellar. Williams gave the electric railway frontage rights in 1907 so they would set aside a four-car spur and flag stop at the corner of Stelling and Stevens Creek. The spur facilitated rail shipments and allowed Williams to receive fruits and grapes from as far away as Sacramento and San Joaquin.

REGULAR AWARD OF
PREMIUMS,
—AT THE—
State Agricultural Fair,
SAN JOSE, 1856.

Farms, Orchards, Vineyards and Field Crops.

Best improved farm, Framed Diploma and $40. J. W. Osborne, Napa.

Fernando, Los Angeles, (olive oil).

Best exhibit of preserved fruit, $10, Genard & Drouet, San Francisco.

Best do of jellies, $10, Mrs. I. Branham, San Jose, for quince, and Mrs. J. L. Sanford, Alameda, for currant, each $10.

Best do of pickles, $10, A. D. Baker, San Francisco.

Best do of catsup, $10, do.

Native Wine.

Best wine from grapes grown in this State, $25, John Froeling, Los Angeles. 2d do, $15, M. Keller, do.

Fruits.

Best exhibit of new varieties of California seedling fruits, $25, Maj. S. J. Hensley, San Jose.

Best specimens and largest variety of apples, $25, John Lewelling, Alameda. 2d do, $15, Joseph Aram, San Jose.

Best and largest variety of pears, $20, Thomas Fallon, do. 2d do, $10, F. W. Macondray, San Mateo.

Best do Peaches, $20, L. Pillier, San Jose. 2d do, $10, A. P. Smith, Sacramento.

Best specimens of apricots, $15, Thos. Fallon, San Jose.

Best specimens of cherries, $15, Wm. Neely Thompson, Napa.

Best do California grapes, $10, M. Keller, Los Angeles. 2d do, $5, Wm. Wolfskill, do.

Best exhibit of foreign grapes, $25, F. W. Macondray, San Mateo. 2d do, $15, A. Delmas, San Jose.

Best exhibit of plums, $15, W. Neely Thompson.

Best specimens of quinces, $20, Major S. J. Hensley, San Jose. 2d do, $10, C. P. Hester, do.

Best exhibit of pomegranates, $20, M. Keller, Los Angeles.

Front page article from the *San Jose Telegraph*, 1856, describes awards given for "Native Wine" at California's first real State Agricultural Fair, held in San Jose.

and emotional attraction. John T. Doyle, Joseph Merithew, Pierre Klein and Dr. John Stewart obviously belong to this group. They came to their second vocation late in life, their families often grown. The common thread that can be seen running through their history, beside their dedication and their success at making excellent wine, is impermanence. A related group whose practical idealism and zeal exceeded by far their capital resources would include such as Paul Masson and Emmett Rixford. And then there were the industrialists, who, seeing a place to invest and make profits did so if their timing and skills were good. Very often, with no previous interest in wine, they quickly faded from the scene in the face of declining profits. This they would see aplenty in the next decade.

Notes for Chapter III

1. George Ordish, *The Great Wine Blight* (New York, 1972); Carlo M. Cipolla, "European Connoisseurs and California Wines, 1875-1895," in James Shideler (ed.), *Agriculture in the Development of the Far West* (Washington DC, 1975), 294-310.

2. *Times*, 5/8/1884, 7/17/1879,7/7/1881, 6/16/1884; *PWSR*, 8/31/1883, 7/8/1889, 6/6/1894; *Santa Clara County and Its Resources* (San Jose, 1895), 205,301; Vivienne Murchie (Portal's granddaughter) to Ralph Rambo, 2/5/1971; *News*, 10/4/1974.

3. Margery Quakenbush (ed.), *County Chronicles* (Cupertino, n.d.), 65; *Times*, 5/9/1884; R.V. Garrod, *Saratoga Story* (Saratoga, 1962), 125-6; *PWSR*, 12/6/1893, 4/30/1904; *Pacific Tree and Vine*, 6/27/1897.

4. *Cupertino Chronicle* (Cupertino, 1975), 10-11; *PWSR*, 7/3/1885, 1/1/1883, 5/27/1887.

5. California History Center, De Anza College, Cupertino, student research papers 77, 1470; *PWSR*, 11/22/1895; *American Wine Press and Mineral Spirits Review*, 10/1912, hereafter *AWP*.

6. Board of State Viticultural Commissioners, *Directory of the Grape Growers, Wine Makers and Distillers of California* (Sacramento, 1891), 132-44. Great care must be taken when using these data. Writers for years have used this work apparently unaware that the community listed was not necessarily where the wine operation was but where the person listed happened to pick up his mail.

7. *Santa Clara Valley* (*PTV*), 9/1887; *Mercury*, 10/25/1895; Frank Norris spent some time at Casa Delmas during the 1895 vintage

and wrote a remarkable description of the activities there, presenting a memorable description of large scale winemaking at that time. *The Wave*, 10/1895; *News*, 4/7/1978.

8. *PWSR*, 5/25/1888; *Bulletin of the Society of the Medical Friends of Wine*, 9/1977; *Mercury*, 1/16/1909.

9. California History Center, papers 893, 1057; Garrod, 130-33; *Mercury*, 8/26/1900; *PWSR*, 11/30/1908; *AWP*, 11/1908.

10. *PWSR*, 2/1/1889, 6/6/1898, 12/31/1899, 8/1900; *Mercury*, 8/22/1900; *AWP*, 11/1903, 1/1910; California history Center, papers 941, 965.

11. Richards, 106-7; *PWSR*, 1/8/1890.

12. *PWSR*, 10/26/1883, 4/30/1912; *AWP*, 9/1906, 10/1908, 9/1915; *W&V*, 3/1937.

13. Interviews by the author of R.V. Garrod, Saratoga historian and California agricultural leader, July, 1968; *Mercury* 9/13/1902.

14. Garrod interview; *PWSR*, 7/3/1885, 1/20/1888; *Herald*, 6/13/1885; *Mercury*, 3/2/1902, 10/15/1907; *AWP*, 3/1908; *PTV*, *passim*, 1896-99.

15. Bruce MacGregor, *South Pacific Coast* (Berkeley, 1968), 123-7; Florence R. Cunningham, *Saratoga's First Hundred Years* (Fresno, 1967), 171; *Herald*, 5/29/1885, 6/4/1887; *PWSR*, 4/20/1892; Los Gatos *News*, 8/18/1899, hereafter *LGN*.

16. *LGN*, 9/10/1886, 1/31/1899, 8/18/1899, 3/29/1907; *Mercury*, 5/21/1895, 12/31/1899.

17. Thomas A. Marshall, S.J., "Early Jesuit Years at Los Gatos," typescript, California History Center; *LGN*, 8/19/1887, 8/18/1899; *Mercury*, 11/5/1892; *W&V*, 11/1921.

18. Harrison, 177-80; *PWSR*, 8/20/1892, 2/22/1890; *Times*, 3/15/1884, 10/5/1884.

19. *PWSR*, 3/27/1885, 11/11/1887, 3/16/1888; *Herald*, 3/27/1885.

20. *PWSR*, 3/16/1888, 9/8/1889, 1/20/1893, 11/20/1893, 8/6/1894, 9/7/1895.

21. Holland, "Bonny Doon Grape War"; *PWSR*, 10/14/1887, 8/6/1894, 9/1900; *AWP*, 12/1910.

22. *Herald*, 5/19/1885, 5/27/1885, 6/9/1885; *PWSR*, 7/22/1895.

23. *Herald*, 3/9/1887, 3/24/1887; *PWSR*, 1/15/1886, 8/13/1886, 1/5/1892, 9/20/1893, 6/5/1891, 2/27/1888.

24. *Times*, 8/14/1881, 9/27/1883, 3/15/1884, 10/5/1884, 6/23/1885; *Redwood Rancher*, July, 1980.

IV. THE DISMAL 90s
DEPRESSION, PESTS AND BETTER WINE

If the San Francisco dealers wish to control the Eastern markets they must pay us a living wage for our wine.
— J.C. Merithew (1894)

You take the list of vineyards in California and run down the names of the vines. It is sickening to read.
— John A. Stewart (1894)

Looking back on the previous decade one can see that the great problems of the 1890s had all appeared for the area's winegrowers well before the 1880s had ended. The chief problem was low prices that began to plague local growers by 1886. There were too many grapes in relation to the winemakers' ability to sell the finished product. Part of the problem was the fact that most winemakers had no outlet other than the great San Francisco wine merchants to whom most of the wine from the valley and the mountains was sold. There it was finished, blended and sold to the East Coast and the rest of the world.

Some leaders here began to argue for a cooperative approach. A huge local warehouse was needed in which the area's vintages could be held off the market until prices were right. There simply was not the capital available for such a project. Then too there was the call for more brandy production to hold down wine production. Brandy was easily stored and could always be sold in a country that loved its spirits. Again, capital was wanting. A great brandy warehouse was called for, but who would finance it?

As economic pressures mounted local winemen more and more understood that organization could apply some relief, even if capital was limited. The Board of State Viticultural Commissioners was established by the state legislature in 1880 and Charles A. Wetmore took command of his brainchild in the forceful manner that would mark his leadership for some years. He was instrumental in pushing the local area to develop its own viticultural society and in 1881 Santa Clara County formed one. Over the years they met regularly. They discussed over production and over planting, disease, and technical winery and vineyard matters. They were often caught up in the heavy

77

political infighting that regularly characterized the relations between the State Board, the charismatic and controversial Wetmore, the professors at Berkeley, and the rest of the industry.

Wetmore and Professor Hilgard both gave much of their attention to Santa Clara Valley matters and the battles between the two, particularly relating to wine quality, tended to divide local people. In 1885 the District Convention of the Commission was held in San Jose, with practically all the living pioneers of the state's industry present. It was a high point for local wine men. Antoine Delmas was able to straighten out Arpad Haraszthy on his faulty history and local winemakers were able to speak out against the San Francisco merchants. It was a lively convention and plenty of good technical material was presented. Many of the technical sessions were actually held in French, still so important was that national element in local wine matters. The scholarly Wetmore promoted the idea and there were but few who complained, mostly those with last names like Pfeffer and Husmann.

Such meetings always brought out the quantity/quality dispute among local wine people. The high quality men were never quite able to get their message across to the standard quality men. The reason was simple. High quality meant planting varieties with lower yields and it meant cultural practises that discouraged heavy irrigation and encouraged closer pruning. It meant fewer tons per acre. Dr. Stewart and Professor Hilgard were voices shouting down the hurricane.

Eastern and overseas markets were also important topics for discussion. Was it better to market wine in the East under your own label or sell it to a San Francisco dealer who would blend it with others and market it under his label, taking away many potential headaches and most of the profits?

Most of the discussions were endemic to the rest of the state's wine industry. But the Santa Clara Valley people had a special problem. It was the quality of the bottom 80% of production. Everyone knew the top 20% was very good. By the 1890s the area had developed a reputation for high alcohol, coarseness of flavor and extreme earthiness. Too many ordinary varieties were grown on heavy, alluvial valley soils. During these years most valley reds were sold through San Francisco merchants and most of these men took it for granted that Santa Clara Valley wines were most useful for blending. Rarely did Santa Clara Valley wine travel under its own colors. Such was not necessarily the case, however, among top quality foothill producers and Santa Cruz mountain winemakers.

Finally, there was the phylloxera, a tiny root louse that probably was brought into the state in the 1860s on rooted vines from France. The pest was not European in origin, however, and had traveled there on American vines where it spread like wildfire. In California it spread more slowly, primarily because the summers here were too dry for the winged female form to develop. This slowness tended to lull California winegrowers into a sense of security. The phylloxera was first positively identified in a Sonoma vineyard in 1873 and did not appear in the Santa Clara Valley until a decade later when it was found in John Auzerais's vineyard east of San Jose. Phylloxera was a problem people didn't like to talk about during these boom times; if the louse were here it would hurt land prices. When it took hold in Cupertino/Mountain View and in Evergreen it changed the history of the entire valley.[1]

THE WINE WAR

Except, perhaps, for the Great Earthquake of 1906, the most dramatic series of events in the history of the California wine industry was the Wine War of the 1890s. The battles and skirmishes captured the interest of the public and were reported in detail across the nation. What captured everyone's interest was the popular image of an economic war between the little guys and a monstrous trust. Actually, it was a contest between two groups of big guys, the California Wine Association and the California Winemakers Corporation, with the local winemakers on the side of the Corporation. The wine makers and vineyardists of the Santa Clara Valley were in the fight to the bitter end.

In the mid 1880s as each year saw huge areas of vines planted, and three years later come into bearing, the wine industry and its leaders were faced with the possibility of depression, overproduction and a huge glut of grapes, wine and brandy. The seven great wine houses of San Francisco, the merchants who bought the young wine from the country and sold it, were very sensitive to this situation and were right willing to take advantage of it. As the volume grew, prices to producers dropped. Wetmore and Arpad Haraszthy both warned the state's winemakers early in 1885 that trouble was coming. In the valley here the leaders could see it coming but imagined it a conspiracy to keep prices down. Portal and Feeley both attacked the "wine ring," as they called it.[2]

Part of the problem was low quality. Unskilled producers who had botched a vintage had to get rid of their wine and would do so at any

INCORPORATED.

AUGUST 10, 1894.

The California Wine Association bought control of as many wineries as possible in California from 1900-1918, dominating the wine scene so that most of the valley's wines produced at this time were under its control.

80

price. And there was lots of bad wine being made in the Santa Clara Valley. Hilgard beat away on this aspect of the situation. If so much bad wine labelled "California" was afloat on the market, prices for all California wine would suffer. Louis Combe, a rising power in valley wine circles in the 1880s, admitted in 1887 that there had been several very large distress sales here the previous year. There was lots of talk in the summer of 1887 of pulling up vines. But 1886 had not produced a large crop and most local cellars were just about empty. When the 1887 vintage started the wine dealers in San Francisco opened with very low offerings for grapes at the wineries they controlled. But by the end of the season a good crop had brought good prices, half again as much as opening bids.

As the Gilroy *Valley Record* put it, when "a few members of the wine interest in San Francisco decreed low prices for grapes . . . at once every little winery throughout the state made their thieving offers even lower than those of the big robbers." This overstates the local situation some, but not much. In the northern counties of the Bay Area, 1887 had not finished so well and after the vintage was concluded there, the St. Helena *Star* grumbled about the "villainous wrong inflicted upon us by the San Francisco wine ring."

Next year there was even more unhappiness. Growers and winemakers talked a lot about unity and cooperation, but did little to effect it. There was talk about other outlets for the crop, particularly drying and making concentrates. 1888 was a big vintage year and grapes averaged $15 per ton, down 25% from 1887. But William Wehner remarked that "times are not bad enough for the average California vineyardist." Poor varieties, overcropping, high sugar — all these meant bad wine and, naturally, low prices.

In 1889 lots of Santa Clara Valley wine grapes were dried. A large part of these were sold to European wine fabricators. There were also large lots sold outside the valley, mostly to Napa's Charles Carpy. The big Pacific Wine Company also did much to handle the crop. The next year Carpy bought this winery and expanded it in order to take advantage of the huge grape supply here.

The gloom and grumbling went on for years. For valley growers and winemakers there was a conspiracy afoot. They would not listen to those who cited overproduction as the cause of the trouble. If such was the case wouldn't prices from wholesalers to retailers have dropped as much? They hadn't yet. Such beliefs were self serving, since any real attempts to control surpluses would mean sacrifices, and that meant money. It would be several decades before agricultural producers

would be ready to control overproduction in an orderly fashion.

A few realists tried to form a Grape Growers Protective Association for the valley in 1891, but at the organizational meeting persons controlling only 1400 acres showed up. In 1892 a terrible April frost and a sizzling September held down the crop and stayed the crash that was coming[3]

The harmful surpluses of California's vineyardists in these years were part of a general agricultural malaise that had hurt American farmers in the late 1880s. Low prices had fostered the growth of regional farmers' alliances and eventually the formation of the Populist Party in 1892. These midwestern and southern farmers also perceived a conspiracy against them in the form of eastern banking interests and the great railroads. Like that of California's winegrowers this perception was partially correct but highly oversimplified.

In 1893 the United States entered a great industrial depression to match the agricultural one it had been experiencing for several years. Now California winegrowers would see that sharp decline in prices to retailers. By the summer of the following year the industry was on its back. Huge surpluses and declining demand hit hard and great batches of wine were dumped on the Chicago and New Orleans markets at prices that returned about three cents per gallon to the winemaker, before expenses. Now cooperation meant survival and in the fall the California Winemakers Corporation (CWC) was formed. In this area practically every important producer joined up. Meanwhile the wine merchants had formed their own California Wine Association (CWA) and incorporated a previously informal relationship into the "wine ring."

For two years these two giant organizations tended to operate in a close and useful relationship. The Santa Clara Valley representatives to the CWC were headed by William Wehner and William Rankin for the larger producers, and Prosper Estrade for the smaller operations. The CWC controlled a large percentage of the state's wine production through its members and sold several million gallons per year to the CWA. The amount of wine controlled by both parties in this process, and the large proportion of the total production this represented, gave CWA the ability to control prices and thoroughly organize the national market. It was the time of the great trusts in America and the wine industry now had its "octopus," albeit a rather benign one.

In 1895 the CWC transferred almost a million gallons of Santa Clara Valley and Santa Cruz Mountain wine to the CWA. The Los Gatos Cooperative put in 225,000 gallons. More typical were S. P.

Stockton with 65,000, E. H. Guppy with 24,000 and J. C. Merithew with 4,000. H. C. Morrell put in 4,000 mountain gallons. This arrangement kept the industry in a fairly stable situation through the worst years of the depression. Wines were carefully graded and poor ones distilled. Higher prices were paid for better varieties. But in the fall of 1896 everything fell apart.

To this day it has been impossible to trace the exact series of events that caused the outbreak of the Wine War. But it seems clear that certain elements in the directorship of the CWC did not play by the rules. Suddenly wines were dumped by "independents" on the New Orleans market. It appeared that certain members of the CWC were better able than others to move their goods. George Husmann wondered if there was collusion between the leaders of the two great organizations. If there had been, it ended in February of 1897 when the CWA brought suit against the CWC for sharp practises and for reneging on their contracts. Delphin Delmas carried the case for the producers and eventually lost it. The CWC was now in the field as a merchant in direct competition with the CWA. Wines were sold at ruinous prices in the East as each side went for broke. The CWC informed its Santa Clara Valley members. "You are fully informed of the bitter warfare that is being waged against you." The *Mercury* cried out that the valley's producers must never again allow themselves to fall into the hands of the San Francisco dealers.[4]

The position of the CWC collapsed in 1898. This was partly due to the growing discontent among the membership and the feeling that certain Corporation leaders were being dishonest. This perception was not unfounded. The Santa Clara producers were the leaders in this growing antipathy. When the CWA won its court case, the two giants tried negotiations toward the end of the year. Paul Masson represented valley producers at these meetings, which got nowhere.

By mid 1899 prices were booming, trade was up, and the CWC, according to William Wehner, was all but dead. Eventually the Corporation sold its remaining wines to the CWA and the war was over.

It should have ended almost before it started, for the country's depression had run its course by the end of 1897, but the two institutions formed to fight the evils of overproduction and cut-throat marketing had attempted to use these surpluses to win an economic battle at the very time that the economy was turning the corner to prosperity. Much that happened during the war can actually be traced to psychological rather than economic causes. When the new century began, a period of almost unbroken prosperity lay ahead for the California wine industry. Markets would expand, prices would never again return to the rock bottom levels of the 1890s. And yet few Santa Clara Valley wine producers who owned vineyards were optimistic in 1900. J. C. Merithew summed it up for many when he reported that in the summer of 1900, vines which bore two tons of grapes per acre in 1899 did not even have leaves. The vineyards of the Santa Clara Valley and the Santa Cruz Mountains were dying.

PHYLLOXERA

The winegrowers of the Santa Clara Valley woke up to the threat of the phylloxera in the 1890s, but too late, by far. It had first appeared on the East Side in 1883, but its spread was slow. Between 1890 and 1894 dropping grape prices and sick looking vines encouraged many growers here to interplant their vineyards with prunes and apricots. As the years went by many simply ripped up the vines as the fruit trees developed. Some on the East Side, like William Wehner, pushed for the use of resistant rootstock, but few were interested yet.

On the West Side the pest did not appear until 1892 and by 1895 there were but patches of it here and there, none greater than an acre. William Pfeffer had been crying for growers to plant on resistants for years, but his pleas fell on deaf ears. Why would anyone in such hard times waste money on such a questionable activity? Many thought the phylloxera was a boon to the industry, a natural way to hold down the oversized grape crops, like killing spring frosts.

Another reason that growers had virtually no interest in using resistants is that the experts in the field and at the University could not agree on which to use. The second greatest gush of polemics during the "dismal 90s" flowed from the various experimenters denegrating the findings of others. Even Professor Hilgard was burned in the battle. He came out early for the use of the native *Vitis californica*, even planted his own vineyard in Mission San Jose on this rootstock. He ended up with a dead vineyard, as did others who followed his advice.

As late as 1895 no one had any idea what the correct answer was. Dr. John Stewart called down from the mountains for Husmann and Hilgard to "stir their stumps." Then in 1896 Arthur P. Hayne of the University's College of Agriculture visited France and discovered what the real problem was. The French separated the various American species into varieties and had tested them separately. This had never happened in California. Here no one had any idea what variety of *Vitis Rupestris* or *riparia* he had. This fact accounted for the

RESISTANT VINES.

VIII.

GUBSERVILLE, CAL., Sept. 9, 1896.

EDITOR PACIFIC TREE AND VINE :

Since it has gone abroad that the University people intend to show photographs of young resistant grape vines, grown during this season from imported French cuttings, to the grape growers of the several wine-growing districts, my curiosity to learn all I can about these Riparia and Rip-Rupestris so highly spoken about, led me to address a letter of inquiry to Prof. Munson of Denison, Texas, regarding the origin of these vines.

As the information received from the gentlemen is of public interest, I request you to publish the same, under date of August 29, 1896. The Professor writes as follows :

"Prof. Hayne, in recommending Grand Glabre and Gloire de Montpellier Riparia for stocks is following the recommendations of best French vine growers based on the extensive experience of the French with stocks. Gloire de Montpellier was first selected by Mr. Louis Vialla, in France from among many other varieties of Riparia obtained from the U. S. on account of vigor and resistance to Phylloxera, and Grand Glabre was No. 13 of a collection of wild Riparia sent from Missouri to France by Mr. Meissner.

These are no doubt excellent in regions having moist air, and deep, sandy, subirrigated soils, but for droughty regions and where deep penetration of root is required they are not so well adapted. Likewise the Rupestris varieties are good in similar situations with Riparia, and will endure in more limy soils, but for the droughty soils, where very deep penetration is required and in very limy and chalky soils, something else must be used for good results. Lenoire and Herbemont are better there, and Doaniana, Champini and Berlandieri much better still. Of these Doaniana and Champini root from cuttings most readily, make plants large enough to graft in one year, and are much longer lived than any Riparia or Rupestris. The three varieties of Rupestris that have given best results in France, and have been named are : 'Rupestris Mission,' 'Rupestris du Lot,' and 'Rupestris Martin.' These all have been selected or developed from among varieties sent to France either by Mr. Jaeger of Missouri or myself. But the climate and soils of California are very different from those of France, and California must do much original experimentation for herself. It is well to try the best varieties from France, and also others from their native habitats in this country, from climate and soil more like that of California, such are the Doaniana, Champini, and Berlandieri of Texas. I have collected many thousands of these for the dry, chalky regions of S. W. France, and have selected and planted a few of the best in my own grounds, and I believe I have as good stocks of all species as are to be found in the world.

They are just beginning to experiment in France with the Doaniana, Champini and Monticola, and some of their hybrids. The Rupestris-Monticola hybrid of which you speak, is one of these, and promises much as a stock. I have one such hybrid that I made by pollinating one of my best Monticola with a splendid Rupestris. The vine is a beauty, a model of vigor, perfectly healthy, it endures intense drought, grows easily from cuttings and in good soil will be large enough to graft in one year ; it grows finely in all soils. I have a few young plants of it which I offer for trial. It is a bearing vine.

If you will take the trouble to test this with several others I am breeding for stocks, I will send you some * * * I am only an introducer, cannot go into extensive growing of stock vines. Your people will soon get a start and then can grow their own supplies. There is no need going to France for American vines, when we have better still at home."

WM. PFEFFER.

Pfeffer, author of this article, maintained a vineyard in Cupertino at the end of Prospect Road which he later sold to Fremont Older. Of German background and well educated, he was one of the leading advocates of experimentation with resistant native wines.

variety of results that people were having with the same species. Hayne picked the Rupestris St. George as the best universal rootstock for California and published his findings in 1897.

The centers for experimentation now were the Napa and Santa Clara Valleys, where several growers had already started trying the St. George. Vineyardists were still hesitant to accept Hayne's advice, but after Professor Husmann visited Paul Masson in December of 1899 and saw the Frenchman's excellent results, the Napa expert fell in line and gave the St. George his blessing.

Within a year everyone had accepted the St. George. Henry Lefranc had imported some grafted vines on St. George in 1898 and had them for sale. Masson himself did a huge business in the next few years selling such grafted vines. In 1903 he actually imported two tons of these benchgrafts to sell in the valley. The prosperity in the wine industry after 1900 meant more planting, and the devastation which everyone could now see convinced most of those doing the planting to use St. George rootstock on which to graft their vinifera varieties. [5]

But nothing could be done about the vines already dying on their own roots. The process on the West Side had been accelerated by three straight years of short rain or virtual drought. This weakened the vines more quickly and the root louse swept through the vineyards from Cupertino to Mayfield. With the growing profitability of pit fruit and the poor conditions in the wine industry, it is small wonder that growers by the scores transformed their vineyards into orchards. Within a mere twenty years the great sea of vines on the West Side had been destroyed. Some were replaced, particularly by vineyardists who owned wineries. In 1901 the Santa Clara Valley vintage was well under a million gallons, less than a third of the total for the mid 90s. The total acreage of vines in the county had dropped from over 12,000 in 1892 to less than 8,000 in 1901. In the San Mateo County mountain vineyards the acreage dropped from 800 to about 200. In the hills above the West Side the phylloxera worked very slowly. But farther south around Alma and Lexington the mountain vineyards were dying by 1901.

For all the bad times there was better wine being made in the Santa Clara Valley at the turn of the century than ten years before. It was received doctrine among American businessmen who survived depressions that such catastrophies were good for the country. They squeezed out the weak, inefficient and non-productive. Faulty as this economic logic was for the country as a whole, there is something to say for it in regards to the wine industry.

Paul Masson at the Bohemian Club retreat in the 1920's. By this time his champagne had attained world renown. During Prohibition he boasted the only license to produce "medicinal Champagne." *(Masson Collection)*

The source of this better wine, of course, was the people growing the grapes and making it. True, there were some different names now, but even when the names were the same, attitudes toward winegrowing had been changed greatly by the experience of the 1890s. Some of the leaders of coming years had weathered the stormy 90s, men like William Rankin and Louis Combe. Others were locals, such as John Corotto and Tracy Learnard, who got their start in these years. Some older operations survived, grew and flourished in later years, such as F. E. Goodrich's El Quito Olive and Vine Farm. And there was a whole new set of French names in winegrowing, attesting to the continued importance of the Gallic influence: Estrade, Gautier, Athenour, Pourroy, Prudhomme, Bouret.

PAUL MASSON

Paul Masson's chief problem in life was the fact that he did not have land or inherited wealth to propel him to the success he desired. What could he not have done in Henry Lefranc's position? What he had in large quantity was his own human capital — intelligence, knowledge, ambition, shrewd business savvy and tremendous energy. His wife's portion of the Lefranc estate was not his and never would be. And anyway, Henry Lefranc was the master there. Masson had to create value in enterprises which really weren't much more than pieces of paper to begin with. His partnership with Henry was a good example. Its success depended on Masson's ability to sell Almaden's products and use his profits to expand on his own. After the partnership ended he continued this arrangement, but he was his own man. Meanwhile he had set up his own good sized wholesale and retail liquor business.

After the good reception of his Champagne in 1892 Masson set about getting it into the public eye. He was able to get the San Francisco house of Bowen & Schram to handle his account and in 1894 had one of the finest displays at San Francisco's Midwinter Fair. Meanwhile he was continuing to push the sale of Lefranc's still wines and opened several good markets for them in Mexico, at Guaymas and Mazatlan, and in Central America. These sales and his liquor business helped generate enough money to develop his newly acquired land above Saratoga.

During the late 1890s he imported several varieties of Burgundy grape vines which would eventually supply a better base for his sparkling wines. These he planted on resistant rootstock on the old Rodoni place. There appears to have been two or three types of red Pinot, the best of which he called his Petite Pinot. There was also

The William Wehner home and vineyard as they stand today as part of "The Villages" development in Evergreen. The huge estate was home for the single most important individual in regional winegrowing 1905-1915.

Chardonnay. Meanwhile he had to search out the best grapes he could find in the valley and foothills.[6]

His champagne did catch on and by 1897 he was wholesaling his "Premier Cuvee" for $18 per case, a dollar more than Arpad Haraszthys famed "Eclipse". George Husmann later stated that Masson's was better because of the better grape varieties he used. Eventually Masson's wine virtually knocked the tottering Haraszthy's off the market. Masson was now able to sell off his liquor business and concentrate on important matters. In 1898 he incorporated his Paul Masson Champagne Co. and made a swing to the East Coast to promote it. He also had been able to line up a huge account with the North German Steamship Company and had somehow managed to provide the only California wine for the 1899 reception for General Shafter at San Francisco's Union League Club.

Masson was doing everything right. Journalist Henry Brainard described his Champagne as the "Pride of California." It was lighter, dryer, purer. He had the best grapes, he employed an absolutely correct "methode champenoise" to produce his sparklers, and he had a remarkable public relations program. He had his vines planted to good resistant rootstock, and was one of the very few in the Western Hemisphere who, before 1900, was employing pure yeast cultures in their fermentations. In 1900 he had 500,000 bottles stored in his cellar at the Hotel Vendome and he was preparing to expand his vineyards above Saratoga and build a great winery there.[7]

WILLIAM WEHNER

If John Doyle had a counterpart on the East Side it was William Wehner. He was a member of a large German family, some of whose members had come here in the 1870s. William was an artist and a successful businessman, combining the two talents in the production of artistic panoramas in the east and midwest. He made a sizeable fortune from this popular craze and in 1887 bought the McCarty Ranch in Evergreen for $20,000, a huge place of 718 acres, mostly hills suited only for grazing, but its western portion dipped down into the foothills. This land was quite suitable for premium winegrowing.

William's brother Ernest began developing the property and had 175 acres of wine grapes planted by 1889. By then William and his large family had come out from Chicago. They built the huge home that still graces the eastern foothills. It has been a valley showplace for close to a century. A large winery was built and by the early 1890s Wehner's Highland Vineyard was producing remarkably fine wine. In

The French community worked together in the early years building up the viticultural industry. These three Frenchmen married daughters of San Jose winegrower Pierre Pellier. Phillipe Prudhomme (left) would run a major retail wine and liquor store in San

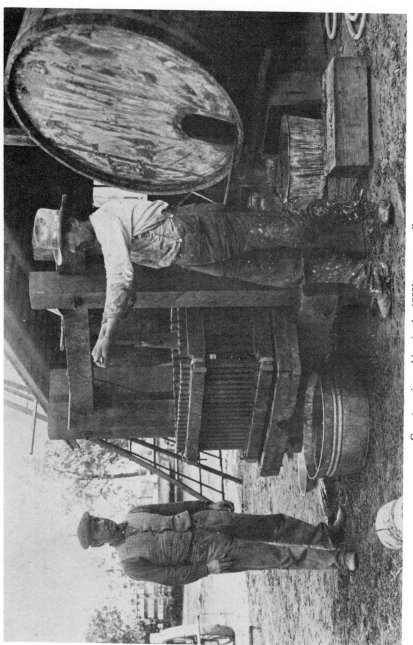

Country winemaking in the 1890's was not all romance.

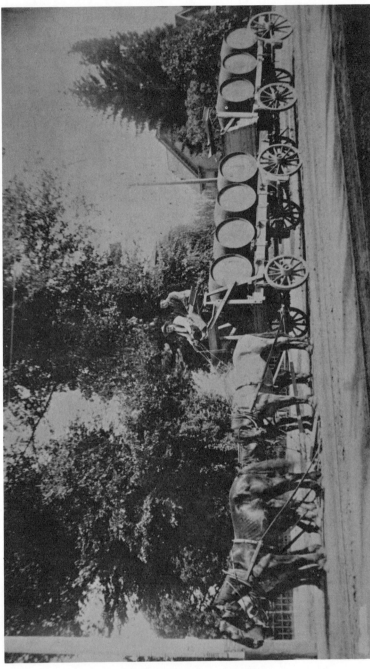

Peter Mirassou (left) and Mr. Spaadafore, winemaker, are hauling wine to the San Jose railroad depot probably for shipment to Winehaven. (circa 1908) (*Mirassou Collection*)

1891 Clarence Wetmore and Arpad Haraszthy both stated that Wehner's Sauterne was the best white wine in the state. He received excellent evaluations at Chicago in 1893 and continued along this line for the next quarter century.

Wehner was an absolute perfectionist. He read widely, kept up on the state of the art and was constantly experimenting in the vineyard and winery. In 1897 he was one of the first to have worked on cool fermentations of white wine. He was an early devotee to planting on resistants, but was one of the few who refused to accept the St. George as a universal. He paid top wages and personally supervised every aspect of his operation. And all the while he maintained his interest in art and culture. In fact, he was almost killed in 1899 when he fell from a scaffold while painting the ceiling of a San Francisco building. He also held an annual vintage festival on his estate which became a tradition over the years.

Wehner took a leading part in the CWC high command during the Wine War, but was one of the first in 1897 to see that their situation was hopeless. He was known and respected throughout the industry because of the remarkable excellence of everything he did. No great calamities befell the Wehner operation while the rest of the valley's industry fell to its knees at the turn of the century. In 1901 he produced 200,000 gallons and within a few years was planning an even greater winery. This he built west of his home in 1908. It is the winery that stands there today, east of the Villages development. Most people choose to identify this edifice as his 1888 winery, which is not the case. In 1915 Wehner sold a large part of his estate to Albert Haentze and went into semi-retirement.[8]

PELLIER/MIRASSOU/CASALEGNO

Pierre Pellier died in 1894 but had been retired from active winemaking for some time. Nevertheless, his family was one of the few that survived the difficult times of the late 19th century and continued to make wine as a family. Pellier's daughter, Henriette, was very close to her father and very much interested in the operation of the winery. In 1874, when his son died, Pellier actually took his fourteen year old daughter into the winery and taught her the business. In 1880 she married Pierre H. Mirassou, who had come to California in 1878. By 1885 the two of them had taken over almost all of the operation of the winery and vineyard, Pellier having retired.

The couple had five children, two daughters, Denise and Therese, and three sons, Peter, Herman and John. Their father's death in 1889

Extensive plantings are seen behind the Leon Renaud ranch home in Evergreen near today's Quimby Road. (*Mirassou Collection*)

Exterior and interior views of Charles A. Baldwin's wine cellar, the present-day De Anza College bookstore. The Miraflores Vineyard produced Bordeaux-style reds, aged in small casks from three to four years. They were recognized for their superior quality in competitions here and abroad.

98

placed great pressure on the family, for the old 1872 debt that Pierre had contracted when he acquired the Evergreen land on the death of his brother Louis was still due Louis' other heirs. The next year Henriette married Thomas Casalegno and he agreed to take over the old mortgage. Thomas and Henriette ran the old Pellier winery for years and as the Mirassou boys grew they took a greater part in the winegrowing operations, particularly Peter and Herman.

Casalegno was active in the CWC during the Wine War and was able to survive due to his early coming to grips with the phylloxera, planting his vineyard to the St. George rootstock.[9]

LOCAL WINE

At the beginning of the 1890s there were no local wines listed on the menu of San Jose's prestigious Hotel Vendome. By the turn of the century this was not so; Paul Masson saw to that. There were, however, just as few local wines traveling under their own labels in 1900 as in 1890. The pattern of distribution for Santa Clara Valley and Santa Cruz Mountain wines did not change much during the decade.

A fairly large amount still stayed in the area and was consumed by local families. It was sold in grocery stores, wine shops, saloons, even door to door, delivered much the same as the milk. Country folk went over to their favorite local winery and brought along their own puncheon to be filled.

Most that left the area went through the cellars in San Francisco where it was blended, usually, with wines of other areas, particulary the reds. During the Wine War most of the local wine went to the CWC. After the collapse of the corporation and the return of good times, the wine merchants, operating under their own labels but still part of the CWA, returned to their position of power. But there was never again the unhappy conflict that earlier marked winemaker/merchant relations. Over the years the CWA was really able to maintain the national market for domestic wines and the result was stability and fair prosperity. It was not difficult to organize the local product in 1900 since it was about one fourth of what it had been before the Wine War.

There were those who marketed their wines under their own labels. E. H. Rixford's La Questa Cabernet Sauvignon was probably the most consistently prestigious wine during these years. Pierre Klein's Mire Valle also appeared here and on the East Coast under its own label. So did Richard Heney's Chateau Ricardo wines and Merithew's sweet wines. Naturally, Paul Masson's Champagne must be included in this category as well as Almaden's still wines. But that historic label was not seen so often as the years went by and Henry Lefranc became more involved in other businesses. In fact, in 1899 he simply sold Almaden's grapes to nearby Estrade Winery and made no wine at the old estate that year.[10]

Although many local wines were produced as varietals, few ever saw market under a varietal name. Even makers such as Doyle and Wehner, who stressed specific varietals as the basis for fine wine, rarely would have their wine marketed under the names of the grapes used. This situation arises from the confusion and controversy surrounding many of the best varietals and their related cousins. There was no better example than the confused understanding of the red Burgundy Pinot varieties. Merchants were also loathe to use anything but the accepted generic terms that had been used in California since the 1860s.

Terms used on the East Coast for years, such as Claret, Burgundy, Sauterne(s) and Champagne, were the words wine drinkers were used to. California wine men, to compete with European products, found they had to use terms that consumers understood. The exceptions were the terms "Cabernet" and "Riesling," which were often used and had good consumer response. Unfortunately, practically anything, including Charbono, could go into a wine labeled Cabernet. And the Grey Riesling grape, no Riesling at all, could be termed "Riesling" in California. There were no laws to control mislabelling of varietals.[11]

One thing confusing wine nomenclature in these early years was the listing of wines and their awards at the various expositions held all over the world between 1876 and 1915, but particularly after 1889. This confusion came from the fact that writers have recorded the wines listed by producers as the items marketed. Very often the wines were entered as varietals or blends of specified varietals. But the fact that William Wehner won awards for his Gutedel, Semillon or Sauvignon Blanc does not mean that any such term ever appeared on a label. In this case the public most likely saw the terms Hock and Sauterne. One reason that California wines could not be entered in foreign contests as Burgundy or Champagne was the use of such terms for non-French wines was considered an attempt to deceive. The French think of Burgundy as a place in France and that the term should be used only on wines from that region.

As far as awards were concerned, valley and mountain producers continued to pile up the medals and plaques. But fewer and fewer of the smaller wineries' names were seen on the premium lists, compared to years gone by. Even some larger ones were not seen, since many were entered under the label of the San Francisco wine house that bottled them. Wehner's great sweet Sauterne won a grand prize at the 1915 Panama-Pacific Exposition, but it carried the Schilling label.

There were exceptions. George Bram took a gold medal at Seattle for his Vine Hill White Riesling. El Quito took one for claret. At the Panama-Pacific Exposition the grand prize for the best claret went to Peter Lint for his Los Gatos Cabernet Sauvignon.

But if there were not so many premium "boutique" producers showing their wares, there is no question about the quality of the average gallon of local wine. We hear no more horror stories of thousands of gallons of acetified plonk being dumped on the New Orleans market. The depression, the Wine War and the phlloxera had sifted out the field. Part of the explanation for this improvement relates to the profound effect of the CWA's benign domination of the industry after the Wine War. There were no hard feelings. Rankin was soon the CWA's head man in the valley and Wehner had no qualms about selling his Lomas Azules wines to the Schilling house of CWA. It was easy to be nice to one another in the euphoria of good prices after 1900. Immigration was pouring wine drinking families into the United States and the demand for sound, inexpensive California wine was rising. In fact, it was time for another planting boom.

Notes for Chapter IV

1. *Times*, 8/12/1881, 8/28/1881, 9/25/1881, 10/30/1881, 1/16/1883, 1/28/1883, 2/25/1883, 3/4/1883, 11/1/1887; *PWSR*, 2/20/1893, 6/6/1893, 8/2/1895.

2. *PWSR*, 1/4/1885, 4/13/1885, 5/30/1885, 6/13/1885.

3. Vincent P. Carosso, *The California Wine Industry, 1830-1895* (Berkeley, 1951), 130-44; Maynard Amerine, "Hilgard and California Viticulture," *Hilgardia*, Vol. 33, No. 1 (July, 1962), 11-16; Guido Rossati, *Relazione di un viaggio d'Istruzione negli Stati Uniti d'America* (Rome, 1900), 147-49; San Francisco *Examiner*, July 1 to September 1, 1889, *passim*. See August 8, 1889 for Hilgard's analysis. *PWSR*, 5/5/1892, 10/5/1892.

4. *Mercury*, 6/21/1897, 7/17/1897, 7/30/1897, 10/31/1897.

5. Arthur P. Hayne, *Resistant Vines*. U.C. College of Agriculture Report, 1896, (Sacramento, 1897); Charles L. Sullivan, "How Vitis Vinifera Got Its Roots," *Redwood Rancher* (July/August,

1981), 16-20; *PRP*, 9/6/1879; *PWSR*, 6/6/1893, 12/9/1895, 12/31/1899, 1/1900, 12/31/1900, 1/31/1900, 2/28/1901; St. Helena *Star*, 1/11/1901, 2/1/1901, 1/10/1902; F.T. Bioletti and E.H. Twight, *Report on the Conditions of Vineyards in Portions of the Santa Clara Valley*, U.C College of Agriculture Bulletin 134 (1903).

6. *PWSR*, 3/20/1894, 12/28/1893, 4/6/1895, 5/7/1896; *PTV*, 4/25/1896. 5/7/1896.

7. *AWP*, 3/1898, *PWSR*, 1/21/1897, 4/30/1902; *Mercury*, 1/25/1899; *PTV*, 11/30/1899, 12/30/1899.

8. H.S. Foote, *Pen Pictures from the Garden of the World* (Chicago, 1888), 532; San Jose *News*, 6/25/1976; *Mercury*, 10/31/1891, 12/1/1901, 8/30/1908; *PWSR*, 11/20/1893, 10/25/1897.

9. Marie Mirassou interview; Eugene Sawyer, *History of Santa Clara County, California* (Los Angeles, 1922), 471; Julius Jacobs, "California's Pioneer Wine Families," *California Historical Quarterly* (Summer, 1975), 154-5; *PWSR*, 12/7/1894; *AWP*, 7/1905.

10. *PTV*, 9/30/1899.

11. Charles L. Sullivan, "California's Generic Table Wines: Their Rise and Decline," *American Wine Society Journal* (Summer, 1981), 34-7.

V. PROSPERITY AND PERIL, 1900-1919

> *The land used in producing grapes should*
> *be allowed to relapse into wilderness . . . ,*
> *pension the men engaged in the wine industry*
> *rather than engage in works the results of which*
> *are disastrous to the Community.*
> — *C.A. Whitney (The Prohibitionist, 1913)*

During almost any year between 1900 and the beginning of Prohibition a casual glance at any of the rhetoric coming from the leaders of the state's winemakers and growers or the leaders of the CWA would seem to indicate that the Wine War was still on and all sides engaged in a fight to the death. But most of it was tactics, "bulling" and "bearing" the market for grapes and wine. The wine interest in the Santa Clara Valley and the Santa Cruz Mountains generally prospered during these years. In the valley it expanded to the south and its industrial nature became more marked. Business was orderly and the great issue of the times was the threat of prohibition. Wine was generally sound and sold well, even though the top 10% in quality was probably not as good as it had been in the 1890s. Unfortunately, this was no longer such an important issue. Prosperity and order satisfied most winemakers and merchants.

SOUTH COUNTY

Between 1901 and 1905 California wine leaders were faced with a dilemma. Prices and demand were strong but the state's grape vines were dying from phylloxera. Each year the yields on older, infected vineyards declined. To fill the growing demand a large expansion of vineyard land was required. But one thing was certain — there would be no more planting binges like that of the 1880s.

The leaders of the CWA knew just where to go in this area. The southern Santa Clara Valley produced good grapes. Soils were adequate. Most of the area south of Morgan Hill had not been transferred to intensive types of agriculture. Land was not expensive and the area was phylloxera free.

There were quite a few vineyards between Coyote and Morgan Hill, and around the town of Gilroy. There were a few wineries in the Gilroy area. The Solis Company served the hills west of town, while the John Rea and Vacca Wineries were in town. These small establishments could not handle the grape production of the area at the turn of the century. Each year large amounts were boxed and sent up by train to San Jose's Pacific Wine Company. The big yields and the good prices in 1901 and 1902 made wine grape growing in the south county a very lucrative activity.

In 1902 several vineyards were going in around the 'San Martin Tract" and in the Gilroy area. Of particular note was a section of 200 acres planted in 1905 by several Santa Clara Valley men. When the vines came into bearing in 1908, the group was incorporated as the San Martin Wine Company. Its purpose was to compete with the CWA and to secure a sure outlet for its own grapes outside "the Trust". It built a winery which it controlled until 1929. The winery was bought by Bruno Filice in 1933 and the Filice family developed the San Martin Winery that became so well known in later years.

The Association moved into the Gilroy area with all its muscle between 1902 and 1905. In 1904 alone they purchased about 3000 tons in the area to ship up to their San Jose plant. What was needed was a local winery with a large capacity to take care of the expanding acreage here. The CWA hired William Rankin to put it together. First he struck a deal with Henry Miller, the western land baron whose home was in the hills west of Gilroy near Mt. Madonna. CWA had already been buying grapes from Miller, over 1500 tons in 1904. Now they agreed to lease Miller's Glen Ranch vineyards and additional land to plant more, totaling 700 acres. They also agreed to purchase a six acre plot on the railroad track north of Gilroy, to build a big winery. Rankin put the whole thing together and in 1905 the $25,000 structure called the Las Animas Winery went up. Meanwhile CWA was offering local growers long term grape contracts at fair prices. Las Animas grew every year as more vines went in and more came into bearing. Virtually all the planting here was on St. George rootstock.

By 1907 wine production at the CWA facility was up to 500,000 gallons. Soon its total capacity passed a million. Even this was not enough to handle the flow. In 1909 the CWA packed up its Pacific Wine Company facility in San Jose and hauled it down to a spot north of San Martin. Until 1919 the south county acted as a giant dry wine factory for the California Wine Association.[1]

Of more lasting historical interest is the large number of growers and small winemakers who settled in the south county in these years. A very large percentage were Italian and they gave the area a fairly strong sense of ethnic homogeneity. Many of these families persisted in their grape growing through Prohibition and started up small wineries after Repeal. Actually, some of these families, particularly in the Hecker Pass area, have had continued importance in recent years: Bonesio, Scagliotti, Bertero, Giretti, Roffinella.

EARTHQUAKE

The California wine industry was never quite the same after the earth cracked and swayed on the morning of April 18, 1906. The fire destroyed about 15 million gallons of wine in San Francisco and all but three of the big wine cellars in the city had been devastated. Out in the country the destruction was not so dramatically concentrated.

Santa Clara County wineries were hit fairly hard. The Novitiate was the most damaged edifice in Los Gatos and to the north several West Side wineries were severly damaged. There was, however, nowhere near the loss that the northern counties had from splitting cooperage. In the mountains the damage was not serious, although one vineyard in the Congress Springs area literally split in two, half of it sliding down the hill. One great mountain casualty was the railroad between Los Gatos and Santa Cruz. The roof came down in the tunnel at Laurel and the line was severed through the mountains. The wine and grape folks here had to do without much of their railroad hauling until January, 1908.

The most startling effects of the earthquake could be seen in the cellars of San Jose's Vendome Hotel where 62,428 bottles of Paul Masson's neatly stacked Champagne had been broken. Masson was doubly hit since his offices and salesroom in San Francisco's Palace Hotel were totally destroyed. But he was now big enough to weather this kind of setback and had over a half million bottles ready for market the next year. The Palace had a great banquet to celebrate its reopening in 1908 and Masson's Champagne was the featured wine.[3]

The wine industry's major changes after 1906 came from the destruction of the great storage and aging facilities in San Francisco. These had grown up over the years and served a very large part of the industry. Young wines were bought in the country, usually in the spring after they were made, and transferred to San Francisco. The mild climate there was good for ageing, certainly much better than that of the hot valleys with their wooden barns that passed for wineries in those days. Well over half the state's vintage was annually handled

After the 1906 earthquake and fire destroyed San Francisco's great wine warehouses, the California Wine Association built "Winehaven" near in this fashion and then sold in bulk under the merchant's label.

In 1906 no one really thought this was the most efficient system, but that was how it had evolved, and San Francisco was where the great cellars were. Not after April 20, however.

The firm of Lachman and Jacobi had already come up with the idea of moving their ageing facilities out toward the vineyard country so that production and finishing could take place under the same roof. They had selected Petaluma, easily accessible to railroads inland and to steam navigation from the Bay. The leaders of the CWA understood the logic and in September, 1906 bought a 47 acre plot of land on the Bay at Point Molate, in the East Bay just north of today's Richmond-San Rafael Bridge. Here a gigantic $3,000,000 complete facility was to be built to handle all aspects of wine production. The crushing facility was dedicated in 1907 and the main plant was finished the next year. From this date a very large percentage of the wine produced in the Santa Clara Valley passed through Winehaven. During Prohibition it was sold off, but still stands almost like new on the Bay today.[3]

The great quake had other effects on the wine industry. There was suddenly a shortage of California wine. This fact forced up prices for about a year, but industry leaders were reluctant to allow these prices to persist. Ordinary people wanted a sound but inexpensive beverage. When prices leaped up, eastern and midwestern "brick vineyards" started pushing their cheaper concocted wine onto the market. Luckily, the Federal Pure Food Law went into effect on January 1, 1907. For the first time it was illegal to place a California label on "wine" made in Missouri or Ohio.

All of this did nothing to upset Santa Clara Valley winegrowers. The south county rejoiced and the drive to plant grapes there in no way lessened. It should not be inferred, however, that this impulse to expand was in any way touched off by the results of the earthquake and fire in San Francisco.[4]

THE PRE-WAR YEARS

The history of the California wine industry in the 1890s, as compared to the 1880s, had been more a story of institutions, trends and problems than of individuals and their operations. The first two decades of the 20th century reveal a history even more marked by this tendency. After the earthquake there were 50 wineries and 11 distilleries in Santa Clara County, but most of the history relates to the activities of the CWA, and to the fight over prohibition. In the Santa

Cruz Mountains the viticultural emphasis turned more and more to the production of table grapes. But when this crop failed or when prices dropped, these grapes went right into the fermenters.

There were still many independents and lots of new names. The Freyschlags at Lone Hill Winery were shipping 125,000 gallons east in 1907 and the Liliencrantz Winery in Aptos added 130,000 gallons of cooperage in that year. The Cupertino side of the industry was becoming more and more concerned with brandy distilling. By 1910 the Cupertino Distilling Company of Arthur Lachman was the chief factor in the area.

The deaths of old timers were fairly common during these years, but two deaths in 1907 and 1909 again changed the course of valley wine history and the fortunes of Paul Masson. The first was that of Frank Moon. He was a wealthy landowner and local politician. But he also was Masson's partner and a major source of his financial backing. Moon was vice president and general manager of the Champagne Company and when he died Masson was able to reorganize his operation and solidify his ownership. In 1909 Henry Lefranc, his wife and their little daughter were driving through San Jose when their automobile was broadsided by an interurban trolley, killing both parents. The daughter, Nelty, hung on to life for several days as the valley prayed for her survival. She lived and was Lefranc's only heir, a fact that placed the Almaden operation quite totally under the control of Masson, although the ownership remained technically in the hands of his wife, her sister, and "little Delmas," as the little girl was nicknamed. (She was a granddaughter of Antoine Delmas.)

Masson did not need these untimely deaths to secure his success. By 1905 he had expanded his Saratoga property, La Cresta, and planted more vineyards. He also finally brought out his Champagne masterpiece, the Oeil de Perdrix (Partridge Eye), a slightly pink sparkling wine made from his Petite Pinot grapes, whose vines he had imported from France. This was probably the most successful single California wine produced before Prohibition. It made Masson's name and fortune. He had also built the great winery that stands on the Masson property today. His winery was built from the stones of the Saratoga Winery, which had been destroyed by the quake, and he had decorated the facade with the Romanesque portal of San Jose's St. Patrick's Church, also destroyed by the temblor.[5]

In 1908 the growing threat of prohibition finally made its impression on the wine industry. Various organizations were formed and eventually consolidated, with directors representing the several

The Mirassou brothers, John, Herman, and Peter are shown with their crew in 1911 as they get ready to plant the vineyard which is home to the present-day Mirassou Winery, Aborn Road, Evergreen. (*Mirassou Collection*)

wine districts of the state. A local Grape Protective Association (GPA) was formed, emphasizing in its name the industry's approach, that is, to stress the grower and his family as the victims of the prohibitionists' campaign. The local leaders of the GPA were E. H. Guppy, J. W. Hicks and John Kerwin. A similar organization was formed in Santa Cruz County. Speakers went through the state emphasizing the importance of wine as a temperance beverage and outlining the economic havoc that would result if the production of wine was outlawed. They were always careful to avoid mention of the importance of brandy and fortified wines in the total industry production. Actually, for some years the anti-prohibition campaign of the wine industry went hand in hand with that of the country's great liquor and beer interests. One man's voice stood out in early years against this union of saloon and wine, Andrea Sbarboro, the founder of Italian Swiss Colony in Sonoma County. He spoke many times in the Santa Clara Valley and eventually brought the local leadership around to his way of thinking.[6]

The economy was fairly steady but in 1908 there seemed to be another depression on the way. It was only a panic, but it scared the wine people, since thousands of Italians went back home when unemployment ballooned for a few months. Wine consumption was hurt and valley people wondered if the south county plantings might have been overdone.

There were also individual events that affected the future. The Novitiate began planting its great Guadalupe Vineyard in 1910. This huge property was located across Guadalupe Creek from Almaden Vineyards and supplied the Los Gatos winery with many of its best grapes.

Out in Evergreen in 1907 the Mirassou brothers formed a partnership with their stepfather, Thomas Casalegno. They built a small winery not far from the Pellier place that Casalegno had run for years. In 1910 they dissolved that partnership, the brothers forming their own and in 1911 purchased 100 acres of wheat land on Aborn Road. This was planted to grapes and today is the site of the Mirassou Winery.

By 1910 the intense anxiety concerning prohibition was steadily growing. When the national Pure Food Exposition was held in San Jose, the local wine industry was not invited to attend. Later in the year the drys had a fit when the winemakers of the state presented 100 cases of wine to the officers of the Cruiser USS California. The gift included a case of Rixford's La Questa Cabernet Sauvignon. There was also a general outcry when the government tried to make the winemakers place the word "type" next to all generic terms on wine labels. In other words Masson's red still wine would have to carry the term "Burgundy Type Wine." The local makers joined the chorus against this regulation, wondering if Vienna sausages and Cheddar cheese would have to follow suit. The government later changed its mind.[7]

To many Californians the happiest event of 1910 was the selection of San Francisco as the site for the Panama-Pacific International Exposition. (PPIE). It would celebrate the eventual opening of the Panama Canal and California wine men set out from the first day of planning to make the industry look its best to counter the prohibitionist tendency. Committees were formed to get everything ready, with Wehner, Masson, Corotto and Rixford the local members.

The good times held and in 1911 the local wine men agreed to an assessment on the number of tons of grapes crushed and gallons of wine produced to promote the anti-prohibition campaign. By now the number of wine grape acres here had risen to about 9,000, well ahead of the dismal days a few years before. American consumption of wine had risen steadily since the earthquake year, going from 40 million to 56 million gallons, although consumption per capita remained steady.[8]

A dark note was sounded in March of 1911 when the California legislature passed a law allowing local jurisdictions to establish their areas as liquor free. For the next seven years the wine industry was faced with an abundance of local option elections all over the state. No small number of the communities and rural areas in this area voted dry. In 1912 Mountain View, Morgan Hill and Los Gatos all voted dry, the latter town being termed by some as the driest place in California. In May a state vote on prohibition was clobbered and Santa Clara County voted 6651-4758 against it.[9]

From 1913 through 1914 the local wine scene became even more stabilized. The Evergreen area was now the dominant factor in north county wine production with about 2500 acres planted and a production of about 600,000 gallons in 1913, mostly white wine. Wehner, the Mirassou brothers and F. J. Smith had the major wineries. Higher up from the valley floor the Mt. Hamilton Vineyard of John A. Koster was making some of the best wine in the area, particularly its White Riesling. Most East Side wine was white and the West Side was predominantly red, with growing tonnages of what was left of flat land production going to the distilleries in Cupertino and San Jose.

An international panel of wine experts (shown here) judged wines at the Exposition. It was here that Peter Lint's Los Gatos Cabernet Sauvignon won a gold medal.

The Panama Pacific International Exposition (1915) presented a grand display of California's agricultural and industrial progress. The "Viticulture Palace" shown above, featured a California Wine Exhibit.

The south county was dominated by the CWA operations, but in 1913 the "trust" allowed many of the local growers to get out of their contracts to sell at higher prices to independent wineries, particularly San Martin Winery.

The outbreak of war in Europe in the summer of 1914 pushed up wine prices and had growers and wine makers smiling. The government laid on a series of war taxes, however, that soon had the state's wine leaders crying, for it included a fifty five cent per gallon tax on fortifying brandy for sweet wine. At first local people were unconcerned, since little sweet wine was produced here. But next year in the Central Valley the conversion of thousands of tons of grapes usually meant for sweets into dry wines depressed dry wine prices and had all producers in the coastal areas upset.

During these months the war itself didn't attract much notice among winegrowers. The prohibition fight was heating up and the opening of the Panama Canal changed a good part of the economics of the industry. Water freight costs to the East Coast were cut by 25%, which made it easier for smaller, independent wineries in this area to place their goods in eastern markets. And as the flow of French wine to the East was cut, the orders for California wine soared.[10] 1914 also saw another prohibition vote in California which was soundly defeated in the state and in Santa Clara County.

A great amount of energy during 1915 was aimed at preparing for the Panama Pacific Exposition in San Francisco. The wine industry put on a great show and local wine producers took an important part in it. July 14 was Wine Day and a great panel of international experts rated a host of California wines and handed out awards by the basket. There were not many local independents represented in the competition, although wines from the valley appeared under CWA labels. Peter Lint received a Grand Prize for his Los Gatos Cabernet Sauvignon and Masson got one for his Oeil de Perdrix. He also received a Medal of Honor for his Sparkling Burgundy. Koster's Mt. Hamilton Vineyard received a gold medal for its Cabernet Sauvignon and a silver for the White Riesling. Rixford took a gold for his La Questa Cabernet as did Wehner for his Sweet Sauterne. That so few local wineries participated is a sad reflection on the pride and competitive zeal here, for the list from the 1893 Columbian Exposition was loaded with Santa Clara Valley and Santa Cruz Mountain winemakers.

The 1915 vintage started on a bad note with a spectacular September rain storm that almost destroyed the valley's grape crop.

The bad luck continued at the Los Gatos-Saratoga Winery when a worker was caught in the crusher and killed. Another worker died in a wine vat at the Locatelli Winery near Ben Lomond.

The great story here in 1916 was the prohibitionists' all out push to make California bone dry. The wine men countered with an extremely effective campaign. Picchetti, Masson, Athenour, Bouret, Estrade, Haentze and Scagliotti — they all took part in protesting"this attempt to destroy our lawful property." Large posters appeared along roads next to vineyards — "Prohibition would destroy this vineyard." [11]

The campaign was a success but had a sobering effect on the wine industry. Sbarboro's advice seemed more and more reasonable, although heretofore many wine leaders had thought it some kind of treason. The wine interest must separate itself, in the popular mind, from the saloon and liquor interests. On December 16, 1916 at the local Grape Protective Association meeting, speaker after speaker called for drastic measures to clean up the saloons. On January 11 the state organization met in San Francisco with a large delegation from Santa Clara County present. They resolved that "This Association is not wedded to the American saloon." Two weeks later the local group formally adopted an anti-saloon resolution. But it was all too late. In three months the United States was at war in Europe and the prohibition forces now had a patriotic basis for their campaign. [12]

THIRTY WILD MONTHS

Being a California winegrower between the summer of 1917 and January, 1920 was akin to a thirty month sentence to Bedlam. Never before had their profits been so great and never had their economic survival been so insecure.

During the summer of 1917 Congress went to work on a Federal Food Bill to help organize the country for war. At first it appeared that no foodstuffs would be allowed in the production of alcoholic beverages, then none for spirits, including brandy and sweet wine. Finally wine was freed from restraints, but beverage brandy was prohibited.

The vintage got under way with huge shipments of grapes heading east in thousands of railroad cars to supply eastern commercial and home winemakers. Prices were excellent; it was the greatest year in the industry's history. But at the end of the season an event in San Jose made wine leaders all over the state gasp. The voters of this city passed a strict anti-saloon ordinance by a vote of 6214-4467. Beer and wine might be served but only with a complete meal in a restaurant or hotel.

San Jose was historically one of California's wettest towns. For many this was the handwriting on the wall. After the vintage the Los Gatos-Saratoga Winery filed dissolution papers. On December 18 a national prohibition amendment was submitted to the states by Congress. Little wonder that fruit trees began appearing between the rows of vines in wine grape vineyards during the dormant season of 1917-1918. [13]

Demand for California wine continued to boom during 1918. Orders from overseas ballooned. Mexico, China, Japan and the Pacific islands all pushed up their orders as European sources dried up. Masson alone had one order for 150 cases of Champagne from China during the summer.

During August local winegrowers took the offensive in the prohibition battle. Congress was now considering complete wartime prohibition. On August 1 there was a mass meeting of winegrowers in San Jose with a telegram sent to California's U. S. senators. Signed by J.E. Mirassou and Albert Haentze, the plea was simple. Don't outlaw wine production! Later in the month an open letter appeared on the front page of the *Mercury*. In it Wehner, Masson and several others argued that the "saloon and the vineyard have nothing in common." The Dry Federation replied by attacking the "'small group of wine growers, masking as farmers." They would destroy the distilleries of Kentucky, the breweries of St. Louis and the wineries of California. Meanwhile the supervisors of the county closed down every drinking establishment in the unincorporated areas of Santa Clara County. As of September 1 only in Gilroy or Alviso could one get a drink.

Again the vintage was a great one. By October 1 there was not an unsold grape in California. Over 6,000 railroad cars full of grapes had been shipped east during the harvest. Another good sign was the government's reaffirmation that heads of families might legally make 200 gallons of wine, free of taxes, for their personal use. That is 1,000 bottles of wine per year, an important statistic for California's wine grape growers.

The end of the vintage was marked by another vote on a statewide prohibition amendment. Again it was defeated at the state and local level. But it was a wild scene. The influenza epidemic was in high season and the negotiations for the Armistice in Europe were going on at the same time. Also, on November 19 President Wilson signed a bill bringing total prohibition to the country until the end of the war. This would take effect July 1, 1919. It must be remembered that the Armistice did not end the war and many, particularly military leaders,

Sign of protest following the Los Gatos vote to be "dry" in 1906. Los Gatos and Palo Alto were the only important dry towns in the valley until Prohibition commenced in 1920.

thought that the fighting would start up again in the summer of 1919.

When 1918 had ended, the statistics showed that 41 million gallons of wine had been shipped out of the state during the year. It had been a bonanza. The Grape Protective Association met on December 14 and advised grape growers to prune their vines and cultivate their vineyards, whatever the law might say. Most took this advice, but hundreds of Santa Clara Valley acres were pulled up during the coming spring. Interplanting was actually more common. Albert Haentze tried to calm the excited growers. He and other local leaders were sure that the government would compensate wine grape growers for their losses, since there was really no other sure outlet for their product. Wine grapes were not like wheat and barley, or table grapes and raisin grapes. R. V. Garrod of the local Farmers Union also raised his voice in favor of compensation.[14]

Flying in the face of the state's voters, the California legislature ratified the national prohibition amendment on January 14 and two days later Nebraska put it over the top. The country would be legally dry on January 16, 1920, one year from the date of ratification. But meanwhile wartime prohibition would go into effect July 1. What would happen to the grape growers?

By now the salvation of the state wine grape growers was obvious. It was the eastern fresh shipments to home winemakers and grape sales to Californians themselves. Everyone waited to see what would happen on July 1. Wilson asked Congress to repeal the beer and wine restriction, but would not act himself. He wanted all the leverage he could muster to get the Senate to ratify the newly signed Versailles Treaty. The more people who disliked remaining in a technical state of war with Germany the better. Even when he came to California the next month to push for ratification, he refused to talk to the winegrowers' representatives.

By now industry leaders were already lining up railroad cars for the harvest. This could be a serious problem, given the perishable nature of the product. By September eastern jobbers were all over the Santa Clara Valley contracting grapes for their customers at home. Paul Masson and Prosper Estrade had sold their vineyard product before the vintage had even started. There were also some foreign buyers in the valley looking for winery and distillery equipment that might be for sale soon. Masson sold off a few large tanks.

There was much talk about alternate uses for the wine grapes. Some talked of drying them, as had been done during the 1890s. There was also some interest in containerizing large batches of juice to ship east for home winemakers. There wasn't the equipment available to consider concentrates yet. The University was much interested in easing the situation. Professor William V. Cruess visited the valley and talked to a meeting of grape growers on alternate products, particularly grape syrup. The host, Albert Haentze, served an ice cream dessert topped off with grape syrup. Several local winemakers did produce syrup, among these, Corotto, Estrade, Athenour, and Mirassou, but it never caught on.

As the season advanced prices skyrocketed. They opened at $30-$35 per ton in this area and were $60 by late October. Car shortages became a serious headache and many tons of grapes had to sit in the sun on sidings waiting for their transportation to arrive. There were also many tons of grapes sold to local people to make wine. Journalist and wine writer Horatio Stoll estimated that 30,000 Bay Area families made wine that season.

And there was lots of regular wine made here, perhaps as much as a million gallons. That at the Novitiate and the Villa Maria would become sacramental wine. Some would be labelled medicinal. Quite a bit would be kept in bond with an eye on the future. [15]

The great calamity had arrived. Prohibition went into effect January 16, 1920. The commercial production of intoxicating beverages was now illegal. They had been since July 1, 1919 anyway. The thing the winemen had been fighting since 1908 had finally happened and profits had never been better.

Notes for Chapter V

1. *Mercury*, 1/15/1901, 6/3/1906, 9/12/1977; *PWSR* 12/31/1904, 2/1908, 6/1909, 7/31/1911; A.R. Morrow notebook, 5/24/1938; Phyllis Butler, *The Valley of Santa Clara* (San Jose, 1975), 178-81; Richard Paul Hinkle, *Central Coast Wine Tour* (St. Helena, 1977), 25.

2. *LGN*, 4/27/1906; *Mercury*, 5/25/1906; *AWP*, 5/1906, 8/1906, 8/1908; MacGregor, 226-29.

3. *PWSR*, 10/1906, 9/1907; San Francisco *Chronicle*, 12/26/1971; Adams, 233-34.

4. *Mercury*, 11/7/1906, 4/21/1907, 10/5/1907; *PWSR*, 9/1906, 1/1907; *AWP*, 9/1906, 12/1906. cf. San Francisco *Examiner-Chronicle*, 4/15/1979.

5. *Mercury*, 2/1/1907, 2/14/1907, 8/20/1909, 8/23/1909; Interviews

with Nelty Delmas Lefranc Horney ("Little Delmas"), August, 1977.

6. *Mercury*, 5/19/1908, 7/19/1908, 8/1/1908, 9/27/1908.
7. Mercury, 1/12/1910, 4/23/1910, 11/15/1910; *PWSR*, 10/31/1910.
8. W.J. Rorabaugh, "Estimated U.S. Alcoholic Beverage Consumption, 1790-1860," *Journal of Studies on Alcohol* (March, 1976), 357-64.
9. *PWSR*, 3/31/1911, 7/1912; *Mercury*, 4/9/1912, 5/21/1912.
10. *AWP*, 8/1914, 10/1914.
11. *AWP*, 5/1916, *passim*.
12. *Mercury*, 12/17/1916, 1/5/1917, 1/24/1917.
13. *PWSR*, 8/1917; *Mercury*, 11/30/1917; Gilman M. Ostrander, *The Prohibition Movement in California* (Berkeley, 1957), 134-48; John R. Meers, "The California Wine and Grape Industry and Prohibition," *California Historical Quarterly* (March, 1967), 19-29.
14. *Mercury*, 12/14/1918, 1/8/1919, 1/26/1919.
15. *California Grape Grower (Wines & Vines)*, 12/1919; *Mercury*, 9/27/1919, 10/5/1919, 10/7/1919.

VI. DRY YEARS IN A WET VALLEY
1920-1933

*The vineyardist is dead. His vineyards
are gone. His income destroyed so far,
at least, as wine grapes are concerned.*
— *San Jose Mercury, 1919*

The day national prohibition went into effect, the president of the Stanford University student body wrecked his automobile on The Alameda. He'd been down to Morgan Hill and had a 40 gallon barrel of wine in his car. Such an event set the tone for the next 13 years in the Santa Clara Valley. Within a few weeks a federal officer here called San Jose "the wettest town in California." He remarked that it seemed the local Italian population had to have its wine. But it is not recorded whether the Stanford student body president was of Italian descent.

All over the Bay Area wineries were raided and many very prominent wine men suddenly found themselves in trouble for having tested the seriousness of law enforcement officers. For the moment there seemed to be a fair amount of vigor to enforce the law. Most winegrowers in the Santa Clara Valley were not much interested in law enforcement. What was most important was getting ready for the 1920 grape harvest.

THE FRESH GRAPE DEAL

A series of rulings and interpretations over the years had legalized the family's right to produce 200 gallons of wine or cider from fruit juices, on home premises, strictly for family consumption and not for sale or removal elsewhere. A passage in the Volstead Act that implemented the 18th Amendment stated that a person might manufacture "non-intoxicating cider and fruit juice for use in his home." The law further stated that ½% alcohol was the top limit on such a beverage. But several court cases and the government's acquiescence generally nullified this percentage. Home winemaking was legal throughout the dry years. [1]

There had been some chaos getting cars for eastern shipments in

1919, organization and order was again being called for by industry leaders headed by Horatio Stoll, publisher of the *California Grape Grower*. In May the California Grape Exchange was set up to bring all elements of the fresh grape deal together and insure the continuation of the prosperity indicated by the 1919 harvest. In March, Stoll and Edgar Sheehan had held meetings in Morgan Hill, Gilroy and at the Union School, near Lone Hill. There were few signups in this area during these early months.

September brought the beginning of the harvest. Early in the month the Internal Revenue Service had indicated the guidelines to be used. Sale of grapes was legal. So was the sale of juice, but not after ½% alcohol had been reached in fermentation. In fact, bonded wineries could continue to make all the wine they wanted, so long as they didn't try to sell it. Several local wineries did so.

The harvest was hectic, particularly when a desperate shortage of pickers developed. But high prices were paid by the eastern contractors and the vineyardists were smiling. Unfortunately a fairly large percentage of the cars arriving in the East contained spoiled fruit, particularly any shipped after the October 10 deluge that swept the valley. Many middlemen were ruined and those who weren't would be much more careful in the future.[2]

Santa Clara County began Prohibition with just under 8,000 acres of wine grapes, a figure that had been fairly steady for a decade. In the spring of 1921 there was a tentative swing back to planting, as 250 acres were set out. It should be noted that a fairly high percentage of all this acreage was interplanted with young fruit trees, as a sort of back up insurance. Santa Cruz County had fallen to 750 acres, but there was a small amount of planting there in 1921. There were still about 300 acres in San Mateo County's mountain vineyards.

The Grape Exchange went to work in the valley with vigor during the spring of 1921, under the local leadership of Albert Haentze. Profits had been so great, however, that many local contractors were competing for grapes as early as June. Paul Masson was among these, as were members of the Cribari family, important Morgan Hill grape growers since 1904.

The grape harvest was another good one for state and local growers. There was still a good amount of confusion and delays, but profits were huge with prices rising to over $150 per ton for selected lots. A railroad strike was threatened, buyers had held back, but demand forced them to buy late in the season at even higher prices than previously offered. The season ended with California having shipped

28,800 carloads of fresh grapes to eastern cities, 5300 more than the previous year. At about 13-14 tons to the car this amounted to about eight pounds of fresh grapes for every person in the country, not counting the grapes used locally in California itself. [3]

Commercial winemaking here was not common, but the Novitiate had a fine vintage. They now had 135 acres of vines behind Los Gatos and at the Guadalupe Vineyard. Their wine was now all sacramental. They made two dry wines and three sweet, but the sweet outnumbered the dry by three to one in volume. Their chief grapes were Malvoisie, Semillon, Sauvignon Blanc, Carignane and Cabernet Sauvignon. All their original plantings had been replaced, having fallen to the phylloxera. In Gilroy, John Corotto also had a good sacramental wine business, selling to Jewish rabbis in New York.

There had been lots of new vines planted in 1921. In the spring of 1922 the number increased. There were about 15,000 acres planted in the state and over 1,000 in the Santa Clara Valley, mostly between San Martin and Gilroy. The Grape Growers Exchange continued its membership drive but could line up only about 20% of the state's growers, probably fewer in this area. The season was much like the previous one with car problems and rain. Several local growers were hurt by the shortage and lost considerably. Even though the Exchange was working on the use of carbon dioxide to cover shipped grapes, over 5,000 of the cars carrying the state's grapes east were nothing but box cars. The Santa Cruz Mountain growers, even though they depended mostly on local buyers, were badly hurt by the rains, with the Zinfandel crop almost totally destroyed. [4]

By the end of planting time in 1923 Santa Clara County had over 10,000 acres of wine grapes. Santa Cruz County was up to 1300 acres. This followed a state pattern. But the rest of the state was not particularly happy at the outcome of the harvest. Cars were short and only 50% arriving were of the refrigerator type. Local growers complained at the end of September that the valley was 35% short on cars.

But Santa Clara Valley came out smiling again. Mildew was terrible almost everywhere else in the state. In some areas mildew and early September rain destroyed the Zinfandel crop, particularly in Santa Cruz. Valley red wine grapes were the champions of the vintage, but there was lots of grumbling here and around the state as prices fell off over 15% from the previous year. The reckoning was getting closer. [5]

By this time a fairly firm pattern of grape varieties suitable for eastern transport had materialized. The demand was overwhelmingly

The Novitiate Winery was established by the Jesuit order in 1886 for the production of sacramental wines. Located above the town of Los Gatos, this 1890's view provides a clear display of vineyards and orchards in the surrounding countryside. The Novitiate is the oldest winery in continuous tilted toward reds. The most popular were Alicante Bouschet, Zinfandel, Petite Sirah (Duriff) and Carignane. The pattern was similar in the Santa Clara Valley, with Mataro also important here. White grapes were a very small percentage of shipments. The most important was the Muscat of Alexandria, used by some home winemakers to soften their coarse concoctions.

The best grapes were those that could stand the trip, and these were not the delicate premium varieties such as Cabernet Sauvignon or Pinot Noir. What was wanted were big yielding varieties with lots of color and tough skins. The result was that many of the state's better varieties were ripped up or grafted over to these better shippers. There were very few acres of top notch wine grapes left in the valley or the mountains. This was particularly true of premium white varieties. One exception to the general picture, was Emmett Rixford's stand of Cabernet vines at Woodside, which survived the Prohibition years. There were a few others, of which the Novitiate was the most important in total acreage. [6]

By the 1924 growing season the shipping of fresh grapes had become established. Some growers were now sending their grapes east under brand names. The state's most famous was the Santa Clara Valley's "Sonny Boy" brand of the Cribaris. Another feature of the market was the growing popularity of the Petite Sirah here and around the state. But its price never equalled that of the coarse and heavily colored Alicante Bouschet.

On of the most important grape marketing operations in the country started in San Jose. David Kellerman had bought 235 acres of vineyard from William Wehner in 1919 and soon established contacts in cities throughout the East. His National F. O. B. Auction Company was headquartered in the Letitia Building in San Jose and growers were invited to come down and watch their crops auctioned off by wire across the country.

In between trips to Europe and his acquiring the only federal patent to produce medicinal Champagne, Paul Masson was reaping great profits from the Salvador grapes he had planted at Almaden during the war. Like the Alicante Bouschet they were "dyer" grapes with dark juice, but the vines were resistant and one could get a crop a year earlier by not having to graft to rootstock. They also ripened fairly early. In 1924 Masson's Salvadors were the first to head east. The state crop was short, but even then prices slumped a bit. There were too many vines in bearing and this number increased every year.

If there ever was a year that should have gone smoothly it was 1925.

The railroad, the Grape Growers Exchange and the State Department of Agriculture had worked out the car situation. Exchange membership was up after a hard signup campaign in the spring and summer. The crop was a fairly good one and things were moving well when suddenly in late October the bottom fell out of the eastern market at a moment when about 15,000 cars of grapes were on track or rolling. At least 10,000 cars weren't even sold. The average price of what could be sold was down another 15%. The last cars sold in New York didn't bring enough to cover freight costs. Within two years 2,000 acres of wine grape vines had been pulled up in Santa Clara County, mostly those previously interplanted. [7]

It was now all down hill for the state's grape growers. Wine grape acreage was up 61,000 acres since 1919, or 62%. The increase in all types of grapes was 102%. The Grape Growers Exchange disbanded in 1926 and was replaced by the California Vineyardists Association (CVA), headed by Donald D. Conn, a bureaucrat who never could escape the realities of the market situation or gain the confidence of the grape growers. All the organization and mass meetings of 1926 went for naught as prices continued to fall. Local growers sold all their grapes but they were unhappy.

The CVA went all out in 1927 to organize the fresh grape shipping. Meetings were held here in May, chaired by Fiore Cribari and Ed Scagliotti. Conn stormed though the valley in August exhorting growers at poorly attended meetings to stick to the CVA. He argued that "overproduction was not the problem," and then agreed that expanded planting had "crowded the field." Again there were September rains and local prices dropped under $40 per ton. When the damage was totalled up at the end of the season, only 804 carloads had left the valley bringing growers about $45 per ton. But half the crop stayed in the valley, going mostly to home winemakers and illegal wine production.

The 1928 season was no better, with prices again falling due to early season dumpings of Central Valley raisin grapes on the fresh market headed east. The election of Herbert Hoover to the presidency did buoy some spirits, for he had promised some relief for the nation's farmers. Coolidge had consistently vetoed such bills. In 1929 the most important event of the season was the merger of the state's major grape products firms into Fruit Industries, a sort of rebirth of the California Wine Association. This merger was aimed at taking advantage of the coming federal assistance seen in the passage of the Farm Relief Act and the establishment of the Federal Farm Board.

126

Fruit Industries also wanted to go beyond the fresh grape shipping. It felt it was illogical to ship all those grapes east every year under tentative market and weather conditions when the product could be delivered to the home winemaker as cans of grape concentrate. There had been concentrate produced throughout Prohibition but Fruit Industries pushed the production and sale of its Vine Glo throughout the country. It was not a great success and in addition the government decided to crack down on its rather blatant advertising and customer service program.

Toward the end of the vintage year the stock market crashed and the country entered the worst depression in its history. If things had been difficult before for California vineyardists during the previous "flush" years, they shuddered to consider the future now. That future was presaged by the specter presented at one point in October when 2800 railroad cars loaded with grapes were standing unsold in the New York City yards.[8]

The depression years before Repeal were marked by the same kind of economic mayhem in the fresh grape deal as dominated the scene from 1926 to 1929. During 1930 there was a massive state campaign to get grape growers to sign up in support of the Control Board established by the Farm Relief Act. It was very exciting, with a necessary 85% signup just making it in early August. Signers and non-signers got somewhat violent, even in the Santa Clara Valley, although this area's growers had made their quota by July 3. At one point the *Mercury* headed a story on the pressures to sign up, "Mobs Threaten Grape Holdouts." There were even stories of night riders and mysterious fires. But the federal relief did little good for the average wine grape grower. Fruit Industries did get a total of $3,555,000 in government loans, one million going to help produce concentrates for home winemakers. Dry leaders hit the ceiling.

By the fall of 1932 the Santa Clara Valley had only about 6,500 acres of wine grapes left and about 300 demoralized growers. Far less than half of the valley's grapes were going east now, the home market here being more reliable. Despite the Democrats' support for Repeal during the presidential year, most growers voted for Hoover, but everyone knew now that the pressure for legalization of light wines and beer would not subside. After the vintage the Grape Growers League was formed in San Francisco to take advantage of this sentiment, with Fiore Cribari the Santa Clara County representative. There would not be another dry vintage.

LAW AND ORDER

The main objective of the Prohibition Amendment was to dry up the nation's very boozy cities. Most of rural America was dry before World War I began. But the Santa Clara Valley was a very special situation. It was a rural area very close to a large and wet urban area, and it had a large foreign population. It was also special because it was an important winegrowing area. Add to this fact the rather secluded character of its many parts, particularly its foothills and surrounding mountains, and the problem of prohibition enforcement is easily seen.

Even under local option, with large parts of the county supposedly dry before 1919, it had been clear that the valley and mountains would not be dry. There was neither the law enforcement energy nor public support for tough enforcement to dry up this area, or even come close.

Not a year went by without large raids on unbonded wine and illegal brandy, some very large. But by far the greatest amount of illegal booze here was whisky produced at secluded rural spots, often next to impossible to detect. The Gilroy area was by far the most fruitful raiding country for wine and brandy. But there were also fairly regular raids in the Santa Cruz Mountains, particularly around Boulder Creek. A good part of the problem stemmed from the large number of corrupt prohibition enforcement officials in the area. This was a particular problem throughout Northern California.[9]

Despite all the raids there were never enough to satisfy the dry forces in the valley or the San Jose *Mercury*. When the incumbent sheriff was defeated in 1930 there was a flurry of enforcement and winery raids all over the valley. But they had little effect on drying up the supplies available to local residents. Part of the problem was the 200 gallons which could be legally made. Only larger hoards were really open to confiscation and fines. There were too many places to make the wine and hide it and there was not enough public sentiment against it, whatever people might think about the evils of the saloon. The illegal wine made in the Santa Clara Valley during Prohibition is still a touchy subject among many old families here. But as one long time winemaker from the Hecker Pass area has said, "We had property taxes to pay and children to feed. The 'revenooers' knew it and we knew it and everybody got along as best they could." In one case two Almaden Valley men were acquitted on the charge of possessing illegal alcoholic beverages, so the 2400 gallons of wine they were caught with was returned to them.[10]

The biggest wine story in the valley during the Prohibition appeared in bold headlines on April 5, 1929. The Paul Masson Winery above Saratoga had apparently been hijacked by a band of desperadoes masquerading as prohibition officers. When the story hit the streets it appeared that the men had tied up the work force and spent all night going through Masson's private collection of rare wines and spirits. On closer look investigators were unable to reconcile the claims with the evidence. The $400,000 heist dropped in value to $100,000. Then Masson re-reckoned it at perhaps $40,000. The Federal Prohibition Administrator calculated $7170, mostly barrels of sherry and brandy. The details of the affair are still not clear but it appears to have been an inside job. Masson may have sold a large quantity of his Champagne to bootleggers, or to certain corrupt law enforcement officers, one of whom was a neighbor. There is also the possibility that Masson may have been forced into it, perhaps as part of a blackmail scheme. There was little concern about it among local folks. The general opinion was that Paul had made a good sale to someone. Suddenly the case disappeared from the press and was dropped by the law. It is still an interesting mystery.[11]

San Jose could have become a chapter heading in the history of Prohibition had a local judge in 1930 ruled otherwise in a case regarding the legality of home winemaking. The federal government had never taken a clear position beyond its rather laissez-faire attitude toward homemade wine, but the matter had never really been settled previously in the courts.

San Jose police had arrested a Willow Glen man when they saw wine barrels in his garage. The district attorney decided to prosecute under the logic that wine was an intoxicating beverage. The judge in the case held that wine was a natural phenomenon. Spirits and beer were *prima facie* illegal, since they had to be manufactured, but wine was nature's work. There is no telling what might have happened had the judge held for the state in this matter. After the finding a Willow Glen magistrate stated that wine might not be intoxicating in San Jose but it was in Willow Glen.[12]

POLITICS AND BOOZE

It was clearly impossible for the tiny force of federal prohibition enforcement officers assigned to the Bay Area to keep this vast region dry. Prohibition enforcement rested heavily on local law officers and to insure that these sheriffs and policemen did their job, dry forces in California made sure that the state had its own enforcement act that paralleled the federal Volstead Act. California got this law in the fall of 1919 before the Prohibition Amendment went into effect.

Taking advantage of the state's intitiative and referendum system, anti-Prohibition leaders circulated a petition that in 1920 put the so-called Harris Act before the voters and for the fourth straight time the people of California voted against Prohibition, this time by a 54% majority. The wine and grape people in Northern California worked hard to defeat the act, and they were successful in Santa Clara County by a mere 400 votes, after a heated campaign in which the *Mercury* had hoped that the law would give the winegrowers "a statutory lesson in nationalism." By now the newspaper had gone bone dry after supporting the wine industry here since the earliest days.

All this left California without a Prohibition law, but the dry forces in the valley quickly pushed through a county enforcement ordinance. This the local grapegrowers went after with energy. The local chapter of the Grape Protective Association (GPA) circulated petitions and got enough signatures to have the ordinance submitted to the voters. The political fight was a bitter one. The *Mercury* insisted that Santa Clara County had to give up light wine and beer to uphold the Constitution. A local Law and Order League was formed to do the upholding and to support the ordinance. This group was clearly nativist in its rhetoric. They made much of the number of Italian names among the grape growers and among those arrested in local raids. They agreed with the state Prohibitionist organ which held that "to the foreign-born leadership, the liquor rebellion looks for its largest support . . . ."It is true that the county's large Italian population gave little support to the idea of prohibition, but the GPA leadership had a variety of national backgrounds. Nevertheless, the grape growers were attacked as the "champions of the bootlegger." The election was a very heavy victory for the dry position (57%) and marked the first time the county had stood in that column. What appears to have provoked the majority was the argument that the Constitution should be supported, whatever a person's personal beliefs. Though not dry in persuasion, the county's voters were still quite conservative and staunchly Republican. [13]

The statewide issue was again raised when the legislature passed the Wright Act in 1922. Again wet forces, with grape growers in the van, forced the law onto the November ballot. This time the state supported the enforcement act by a mere 52%; Santa Clara County's support level was 54%. Two years later an initiative was circulated by the GPA and again the Wright Act was put to the voters, with about the same results. (However, if Los Angeles's totals were subtracted, the Wright Act would have died.) Santa Clara County again voted for law and order, this time by 58%. It was the only important winegrowing County in Northern California to support the enforcement act. Napa County voted to dump the Wright Act by 61%.

This ended the GPA's attempts to undo Prohibition at the state and local level. It was not until Repeal seemed almost inevitable, in November of 1932, that the Wright Act was again attacked. This time, on the same ballot as the Roosevelt-Hoover contest, the enforcement act was swamped by 800,000 votes. Santa Clara County's voters approved of its demise by 61%, although Roosevelt barely nipped Hoover in the local vote. This left the county's "Little Volstead Act" on the books and in force until April, 1933 when Congress legalized beer and something called "3.2%" wine.

Notes for Chapter VI

1. Ostrander, 178.
2. *W&V*, 2/1920, 3/1920; *Mercury*, 3/24/1920, 9/16/1920, 9/18/1920, 9/26/1920.
3. *W&V*, 10/1921; *Mercury*, 11/24/1921; L.D. Mallory, et al, "Factors Affecting Annual Prices of California Fresh Grapes, 1921-1929" *Hilgradia* 6:4 (September, 1931), 111-23.
4. *W&V*, 4/1922, 7/1922; *Mercury*, 9/30/1922, 10/20/1922.
5. Mallory, 113; *Mercury*, 9/25/1923, 10/12/1923; *W&V*, 11/1923.
6. Charles L. Sullivan, "Prohibition and California Wine," *Society of Wine Educators Newsletter* (Spring, 1981), 4-5; Horatio F. Stoll, *California's Most Important Juice Grape Varieties* (San Francisco, 1925), 5-23.
7. *W&V*, 6/1925, 11/1925; *Mercury*, 10/17/1925.
8. Leon D. Adams, "Revitalizing the California Wine Industry." University of California, Berkeley. California Wine Industry Oral History Project, 1974, 15-33; *Mercury*, 7/27/1926, 5/12/1927, 10/5/1928, 7/17/1929, 10/15/1929; *W&V*, 7/1929; Ostrander, 179.
9. R.A. Kelley, *Liberty's Last Stand* (San Francisco, 1932); Interviews with Eleanor Ray, widow of Martin Ray, March, 1979; Garrod interviews; Ostrander, 169-81.
10. Richard Paul Hindle, *Central Coast Wine Tour* (St. Helena, 1977),

182; *Mercury*, 10/18/1928, 4/4/1931, 3/8/1932.

11. Charles L. Sullivan, "The Day They Robbed Paul Masson," *Vintage* (July, 1979), 20-28; Eleanor Ray interviews; Garrod interviews; *Mercury*, 4/5/1929, *passim*.

12. *Mercury*, 5/2/1930, 6/21/1930.

13. *California Liberator*, 6/22/1922, 6/1931; *W&V*, 12/1920; *Mercury*, 11/1/1921.

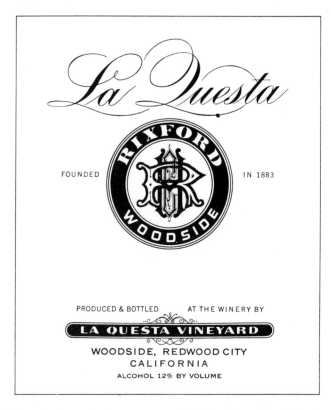

E.H. Rixford's Cabernet Sauvignon was one of California's most prestigious brands by 1900. Formally located where Highway 84 intersects Highway 280, the grapes are still cultivated and used by Robert and Polly Mullen's Woodside Winery.

VII. REPEAL/RECOVERY/RELOCATION
1933-1960

Around the edges of the valley there are
a good many thousand acres admirably adapted
to the growing of the vine. The foothills of
the Santa Cruz Mountains are even better.
They could be, and perhaps someday will be,
one great vineyard.

— Frank Schoonmaker (1941)

The 1932 vintage was an exciting one in the Santa Clara Valley. This year even fewer local grapes went out by railroad. By now most people here were sure that the dry days were numbered and the local fermenters were loaded up, in bonded and unbonded wineries. By the end of the season the election results had vouchsafed this view. The Wright Act was dead, Roosevelt had won on an "end Prohibition" platform, and the next Congress would be wringing wet.

REPEAL

The "lame duck" Congress that met after the election would do nothing about changing the Volstead Act. California's new U. S. Senator, William Gibbs McAdoo, wrote House Speaker John Nance Garner that his state's grape industry was *"in extremis"*. And the orators lined up in Congress to argue that "the old wine decanter should be restored to the dinner table." But the wet forces could get nothing concrete. Nevertheless, the old Congress did submit the 21st Amendment to the states. This would nationalize Repeal.

When the new Congress met in March they could do nothing about the Constitution, but they could re-define the meaning of "intoxicating beverage." It was understood from the outset that this meant legalizing beer and light wine. Now it transpired that Democractic Congressmen, many from non wine drinking states, couldn't figure out why beer should be legalized at 3.2% while wine got a higher figure. It seemed downright unfair to many of the Southern committee chairmen. California winegrowers wrung their hands in despair as Congress went ahead and legalized beer *and* wine with a maximum of 3.2% alcohol. What hurt even more was the fact that Senator McAdoo apparently went along with this nonsense. But anyone who looked back at his attempts to get the Democratic presidential nomination in 1924 as the darling of the drys should not have been surprised. California wine men called the strange stuff produced under this regulation "McAdoo wine."[1]

The Amendment submitted to the states called for the popular election of delegates in each state, these to meet in conventions. They were paired off dry-wet in the elections and California again came in solidly on the wet side. Santa Clara County voted 71% for wet candidates, with every area voting to end Prohibition, even Palo Alto, which had been in the dry column since 1914. The San Jose *Mercury* growled angrily at the results.

With Prohibition doomed the 1933 vintage was even more clearly directed to the production of wine in this area. Carload shipments of fresh grapes were still huge, but these came mostly from the Central Valley. There were, perhaps, 2,000,000 gallons of wine stored in the county before the vintage, a good part of it produced in 1932. In 1933 Santa Clara County made another 3,000,000 gallons, bringing the total here to well over a third of all the dry wine in the state waiting to move to consumers. During the month of November about 100,000 gallons were shipped east under bond, to get ready for Repeal, which came in December. Now a remarkable situation occurred, Bonded wineries had to wait to receive their excise stamps before they could sell any wine. Unbonded, so-called "bootleg" wineries, could sell their wine right away, simply by buying a $59.34 federal tax stamp. There were a few weeks here when some of the larger winery owners gnashed their teeth as the little fellows marketed their goods.[2]

TOOLING UP

The main problem of the local winery owners was getting their equipment in proper order and expanding facilities. The depression was still very severe and credit was still a problem. Some had been able to move early. The Cribaris had put their big Madrone Winery into shape and the Bisceglias had taken over the Wehner Winery and had been tooling up here and at the huge Greystone Winery in Napa Valley, which they also controlled. Bruno Filice had sold his grocery business to be able to concentrate his resources on the San Martin Winery.

The Cribaris put the Madrone Winery right into the production of

3.2% wine in the spring of 1933 and were shipping it out in June at a rate of 10,000 gallons per week. At Repeal they had about 500,000 gallons of regular wine on hand and had raised their capacity to about 1,000,000 gallons. Madrone produced a claret from Mataro, Mission and Aramon grapes, and a Burgundy from Carignane, Malvoisie and Petite Sirah. They also had a Zinfandel, Cabernet and Barbera, giving their winery a solid dry wine slant. The San Martin Winery's capacity was raised to 500,000 gallons. They made 25,000 gallons of dry and 100,000 gallons of sweet during the next season.

The Novitiate was ready to go when Repeal came and had made lots of wine in the 1933 vintage. Bad luck, or possibly an arsonist, struck in December, however, and the winery was destroyed. Casks of old Port and sherry split open. The wine and water from the hoses ran into a large cistern. Some of it was used to help fight the fire, but 200,000 gallons of Angelica, Burgundy and claret were saved. By the next April the building of a new winery was well under way and was ready for the next vintage. It soon had a 500,000 gallon capacity with 128,000 of that in oak. Novitiate also began expanding their vineyards, having bought the 1200 acre Tevis estate in the hills above Lexington.

The big wine news in the valley came in the summer of 1930 when Paul Masson announced that he was selling the Almaden Winery and vineyards. Actually he traded them for the 26,153 acre Orestimba Ranch east of Gilroy, which he then leased to a Southern California concern. Shortly thereafter a group of businessmen headed by Charles M. Jones formed the Almaden Vineyard Corporation and purchased the old winery and 350 acres. Masson had made wine there during Prohibition, some as part of the base for his sparkling wine and some for the day he knew would come when his beloved product was again a legal beverage. Jones claimed that there were about 1,000,000 gallons of dry wine on hand at Almaden at Repeal, perhaps the largest collection of high grade dry table wine in California. The company hired Jack Wetmore the son of the late great Charles A. Wetmore as winemaker and started right away with the production of their Maison Rouge and Maison Blanc table wines, which became very popular. Paul Masson was somewhat upset at this choice of trade name, for he felt the new owners were playing on his own. He announced that he was now in retirement, but brought out his 1929 Oeil de Perdrix, which had been produced under bond and under his permit to produce Champagne for medicinal purposes.

When Albert Haentze's Villa Vista wines are added to those mentioned above, the entire list of brand name wine in the Santa Clara

Valley shortly after Repeal is complete. Of course, there were many other wineries operating, 64 of them by 1936. Most of these were bulk operations, small family affairs that sold wine at the winery in anything from a corked and labeled bottle to a 50 gallon barrel. The rest was sold to other wineries. Some were fairly large, such as the Athenour Brothers Winery and Gregory Bouret's Neuchatel Vineyard, both off Branham Lane where the valley's viticultural roots were set. Elena Puccinelli's winery north of Los Gatos could hold 62,000 gallons and made 35,000 in 1934. Charles Rousten and the Picchettis started up in the Montebello district as did Eloi Pourroy near Congress Springs. The Cupertino/Mountain View wine district was about dead, but an important winery was opened near the El Camino Real in Mountain View by John Gemello in 1934. He had worked in the area's wineries and vineyards long before prohibition. Farther north at Woodside Emmet Rixford's sons, Halsey and Allan, made La Questa Cabernet Sauvignon for a few years.

Farther back in the Santa Cruz Mountains, Emil Meyer's Mare Vista Winery started back into production, making 6,000 gallons in 1935. By the next year there were nine wineries in Santa Cruz County. The Locatelli Winery on Eagle Rock Ranch, northwest of Felton, was run by the family that had taken over the Ben Lomond Wine Company's vineyards at Bonny Doon before World War I. And near Soquel, below Santa Cruz, John Bargetto opened a new operation that would have a long history. In all, there were about 1200 acres of wine grapes in Santa Cruz County at the end of Prohibition, but many of these vines were in sorry shape. Quite a few of the newer plantings had been around Watsonville to supply local home winemakers. These were soon pulled out. Santa Clara County's total held fairly steady after the late 1920s at about 7,000 acres, 1900 of which were Zinfandel. Most of the new planting in both counties after Repeal was to white grapes, since there had been little demand for them during Prohibition and the entire state was woefully short of good white varieties.

It was soon clear that sweet wines were where the country's demand lay. This was difficult for the Santa Clara Valley, traditionally a dry wine area. The valley had few distilleries that could produce the fortifying brandy to make sweet wines. Bisceglia and Cribari had large ones, as did the Novitiate. But that was all, except for the tiny still the Jesuits maintained at the Villa Maria. Its 193 gallon capacity wouldn't help much. For some time fortifying brandy had to be imported into the valley.

Most of the wineries and vineyards were to be found in the southern part of the county. There were several old timers in the Hecker Pass area who had started up again: Bonesio, Scagliotti, Giretti. There were also some new ones here and in the valley proper: Conrotto, Pappani, Guglielmo. These would last. Others started up but did not last: Godani, Carpignano, Giacchino, Monaco. It should be clear from the names of these owners that the Italian influence in south county winegrowing was even more pronounced than before Prohibition.

THE NEW INDUSTRY

The new California wine industry had a very different point of view and leadership than its counterpart before Prohibition. Because of the great demand for fortified and sweet wines, Central Valley wine producers had an extremely powerful voice in the industry. This tilt toward sweet wine tended to put a very large part of the industry in the hands of people who were more concerned with disposing of the giant California grape crop than with how good California wine was. The hotbed of concern for wine quality and devotion to wine as an important part of life was the North Bay winegrowing area and the Livermore Valley. The Santa Clara Valley had a rather split personality, split in several ways. An important part of the production was country wine for local consumption, some quite good and some simply awful. There was also a very powerful industrial element, represented by the Cribaris, Bisceglias and Filices. These large wineries had similar motivations as the large Central Valley plants, but they did not sit in the great sea of table and raisin grapes found in Fresno County, so that their commitment to good wine was a bit more serious than that of the producers in the Fresno area. There were also the few who hoped to reestablish a premium tradition here. In the long run they and the capable country wine producers prevailed. The industrialists moved to the Central Valley.

The sweet wine tilt in the consumption of California wine was truly remarkable. In 1935 the ratio of sweet to dry California wine consumed was about 3:1. Before Prohibition it had been more like 2:3. And yet the national consumption of sweet wine per capita had hardly changed since World War I. The problem was that a large percentage of dry wine drinkers had been making their own wine and were continuing to do so. Approximately 23,000,000 gallons of homemade wine were produced the year after Repeal. Another very important factor in the industry's new condition was that in 1935 fully 44% of all California wine was consumed in California. Consumption was 3.36 gallons per capita, almost ten times the national average.

Ed (left) and John Pedrizetti are important for their Morgan Hill winery developed in the 1940's and still operating on San Pedro Avenue.

The effect of this tilt on Santa Clara Valley operations can be seen in the 1936 production figures. Only 58% of the local production was dry, totally out of character compared to pre-Prohibition years.[4]

Some examples of local wine shipments here during the first six months after Repeal: Cribari (58,000), Almaden (37,457),San Martin (11,300), Novitiate (11,506), Puccinelli (8,360),Bouret (11,584), Bertero (6,579). The Bisceglia operation shipped almost 500,000 gallons, but this figure includes wine from other areas,

The New Deal's concern for agriculture was another problem for the new wine industry. Codes, marketing orders, regulations all had to be hammered out, usually with wine people taking part in the discussions. Winegrowers were also concerned with the industry's relationship to the new Agricultural Adjustment Administration. Local leaders met with Adlai E. Stevenson when he came through in 1934 as the assistant general counsel of the Federal Alcohol Control Administration. But perhaps the best thing the New Deal did for California's winegrowers, besides Repeal, was Mrs. Roosevelt's firm determination to serve only this country's wine at the White House and the President's obviously cordial attitude toward California wine.

Another new industry feature was the Wine Institute, formed in 1934 to promote the industry and to improve wine quality. By 1935, 83% of all the wine produced in the state came from Institute members, who paid an assessment to the organization in relation to production and sales. There was a fairly good memberhsip from this area. The early lists show Almaden, Haentze and Bisceglia but Cribari and San Martin were missing. Novitiate and even Villa Maria were early members. Most of the smaller country wineries did not join, but Anselmo Conrotto was an exception in the south county. The only member from the mountains was Mare Vista. The local members of the Wine Institute's Board of Directors were Almaden's Charles Jones and Alphonse Bisceglia.

Symbolic examples of rebirth in the 1930s were also evident. California wines appeared in the best hotels as they never had before Prohibition. Most were from North Coast wineries, but Almaden Maison Rouge and Maison Blanc could be found at San Francisco's Palace and Fairmont. Paul Masson's Champagne, of course, was everywhere fine wine was served, at $5.00 per bottle. The industry's association with the State Fair was also revived. Many wineries entered their wares from the first, but one searches in vain for Santa Clara Valley or Santa Cruz Mountain wines on the earliest premium lists. Nevertheless, local winegrowers who had lived through the ugly

Prohibition battles before 1919 had to smile when the San Jose Rotary Club honored the valley's wine and grape men in April, 1934. It had been quite a struggle.[5]

The years before the war brought several important changes to the valley's wine industry. In 1941 the Cribari family gained control of the old Wehner Winery, the home and Villa Vista Ranch next door. Paul Masson had died the year before. He was then in real retirement, for he had sold the Champagne Company in 1936 to Martin Ray, a local businessman and stockbroker who had acquired a keen interest in fine wine and a very strong attachment to the person of Paul Masson. Martin Ray believed that the lands of the Chaine d'Or had unsurpassed potential for the production of premium wines. The story goes that Masson did not want Ray to buy his place, but to establish his own vineyards on higher land to the north, and that Ray was able to acquire the property through the offices of a third party.

In 1940 he established his "Martin Ray System" for marketing his premium wines under the Paul Masson label. He established vintage prices on Thanksgiving Day and until Christmas one might sign up for wine, with delivery three or four years later. Payment was 50% in advance. It was the "futures" system that has occasionally been popular in recent years. At this time Ray was producing about 2,000 cases of still wine and 3,000 of Champagne. All this came to a bitter end on July 7, 1941, when the Masson Winery was destroyed in a terrible fire.[6]

Local folks interested in the wine world at that time had an excellent source of information in the Santa Clara Valley. Robert Mayock, a native of Gilroy, had acquired the old Los Amigos Winery (Grau and Werner) near Mission San Jose. Mayock producd an excellent wine and ran a wine and food column in the San Jose *Evening News* starting in 1940 and running through the war to September, 1945. There was chit-chat on local wine matters and people in the industry and was one of the first of its kind in California. One might read about the local organization for wine fanatics called the Sauterne Club. Here wine men like Cribari, Filice, Bouret, Mirassou and Mayock met and drank good wine, and talked about it a lot. On one occasion Maynard Amerine, a San Jose native son, was the Club's guest. He had already begun to make a name for himself as a professor on enology at the University.

In 1937 an important new winery was founded in Evergreen. Actually it was the rebirth of winemaking in a family that had been valley pioneers in the industry. After World War I the partnership of

Early photo of the crush at the Pellier-Mirassou ranch in Evergreen. Men with pitch forks (center) will be loading the stems and leaves into wagons for reuse as fertilizer in the vineyard.

By 1917, Mirassou no longer transported its wine in puncheons to Winehaven, but loaded it into tank cars at what is today the spur track of Southern Lumber, at 1st and Alma, San Jose. (*Mirassou Collection*)

143

the three Mirassou brothers was ended. John and Herman acquired land elsewhere in the valley and Peter kept the 100 acres they had previously purchased and planted to vines. Peter Mirassou worked this land through Prohibition, selling his grapes to others for wine and taking a leading position in the valley's grape grower organizations. This pattern continued until the family determined to go back into the winemaking business after a layoff of 18 years. Peter and his two sons, Norbert and Edmund, had built a 130,000 gallon winery in the spring and summer of 1937, which was ready for the vintage that year. For some years the Mirassou Winery was strictly a bulk operation, selling their product to other wineries. They planted better varieties and developed a bulk product that was quite a cut above that of most such operations. They also produced high quality Champagne stock for others' production. In 1941 they hired Max Huebner, who in the years to come helped bring an even sharper premium focus to the Mirassous' winery. Peter Mirassou lived on until 1951, but most of the energy in developing the winery in these early years came from his sons.[8]

There were also changes at Almaden. In the summer of 1941 San Francisco businessmen Louis Benoist and Brayton Wilbur bought Almaden from the Jones estate. They also brought in Frank Schoonmaker to help give direction to the new owners' interest in high quality wines. Schoonmaker had recently written a book on American wine in which he excoriated many California winemakers for using poor grapes and making improperly labeled, rather ugly wine. He had praised a few and had special plaudits for the foothill areas around the Santa Clara Valley. Also hired by Benoist was Oliver Goulet, who had previously been winemaster at the Novitiate and had been working for Martin Ray. The Benoist/Schoonmaker/Goulet triumverate at Almaden lasted over twenty years.[8]

WORLD WAR II

United States entry into World War II in 1941 eventually did much to alter the operations of the state's wine industry. But this time the effect was not as great as that of entry into the Great War; this time there was no serious threat from the prohibitionists. There were about 8,000 acres of wine grapes in the Santa Clara Valley and these equalled about 12% of all such acreage in the premium coastal counties of Northern California. These figures changed little during the war years. But the number of bonded wineries dropped from 55 to about 40.

Santa Clara County production during the four war vintages

144

averaged about 2,700,000 gallons. Dry reds were still predominant, coming to about half the total. There were also about 500,000 gallons of dry white wine and 800,000 gallons of sweet each year. For the state at large sweet wine led dry by more than two to one.

The industry's leaders remembered World War I well and made no such public relations gaffs as had characterized much of the wet rhetoric before. The production of beverage brandy was cut to almost nothing and the amount going to fortify sweet wines was also held down. There were few public complaints from the wine men. One thing that helped matters was the governments's insistance that raisin grapes be used to produce raisins instead of cheap wine. Thus, the annual dump of surplus raisins into Central Valley fermenters did not take place. Nevertheless, the government's Office of Price Administration and the War Production Board did not allow grape or wine prices to advance much. In fact, the price controls on grapes and on finished wine were not always in logical relationship. One year fresh grape prices were allowed to move up sharply, but wine prices were maintained. There was some grumbling over that situation.

To the industry's ultimate advantage a serious tank car shortage developed early in the war, meaning that wineries could not so easily ship bulk wine east. The solution was more bottling in the state and at the winery. This started a trend that was never reversed. Eastern bottlers complained, but the larger ones just bought up several California wineries for themselves, particularly in the Central Valley. Lots of wine went east in tank cars after the war, but by the 1950s it had declined to a dribble. California winemakers, such as Cribari and San Martin here, took pride now in telling the public about their wines that had been "bottled at the winery."

Much of the distilling in the state ended, of course, and a large amount of Central Valley equipment was sent east where it could work year round. That which did remain was used in the off season to make industrial alcohol from molasses. Cribari and San Martin did some of this work. Part of this activity was aimed at synthetic rubber production.[9]

One of the most significant developments in the wine industry resulting from the war was the purchase of 25% of the industry by large national distillers. Most of these purchases were of large scale bulk operations, but in 1943 Joseph E. Seagram & Sons purchased the Paul Masson Champagne Company from Martin Ray. Ray had done much to rebuild the operation after the disastrous 1941 fire, but now he decided to take advantage of the situation and accept the Seagram offer. He would follow Masson's advice and start anew on the Chaine d'Or mountains to the north. Seagram made wine for the next two years but did not market it. The company sold a portion of its interest to a firm headed by Alfred Fromm and Franz Sichel in 1945, but maintained a silent majority interest in Masson. In general the distillers got rid of their winery properties after the war, but the Seagram decision to hold on to Masson paid off handsomely in years to come.[10]

There was a fairly continuous shortage of California wine through the war, despite the fact that about 35,000 acres of grapes were planted. But few of these were to good wine varieties. One good planting took place at Almaden. Starting in 1942 the new ownership began a ten year planting program, stressing the varietals that Schoonmaker had been advocating.

1942 was also the year that Almaden brought out its first Champagne, the "Extra Dry." Schoonmaker's contributions can also be seen in the appearance of Almaden's Grenache Rose, which also appeared that year. This wine was unique in the industry and established an important trend. (Schoonmaker was soon off to the war, serving in Europe with the OSS.)[11]

One wouldn't have thought there was a wine shortage in 1943 to read the California wine list at New York's Waldorf Astoria Hotel. There were 79 California wines listed, with several from the Santa Clara Valley. Almaden was represented by its Champagne and Grenache Rose. The Novitiate had a Burgundy and its Chateau Novitiate sweet Sauterne. Cribari had a Sauterne, a white Burgundy and a red Burgundy. Paul Masson's prewar wines led the list from this area. There was a Cabernet Sauvignon, a Pinot Blanc Vrai, a Pinot Chardonnay, Gamay Beaujolais, and, of course, a 1936 Brut Champagne.[12]

Just before the war ended Edmund Rossi, one of the industry's greatest leaders, truly devoted to the development of fine table wine as a part of American life, made some remarkable predictions. During the next 25 years the industry would see a great rise in the production and consumption of good table wine, surpassing dessert wine. There would be much higher quality, even some really superlative wines produced. More of the right grapes would be grown in the right places. Americans had a sweet tooth for wine now, but with education they would become dry wine drinkers. This education had already begun at the Wine Institute and the Wine Advisory Board. The Leon Adams Wine Study Course was already available from the Institute, aimed at both consumers and people inside the industry. It would be 23 years from Rossi's address that table wine consumption passed dessert wine in the United States. There were still many years of hard work ahead, years that might have seemed as if the industry was running in place.[13]

RUNNING IN PLACE

Two important stories emerge from an examination of the winegrowing history in the South Bay counties after the war and during the 1950s. One is the re-establishment of the area as a premium region of wine production through the remarkable efforts of the larger operations in the Santa Clara Valley. The other is the re-establishment of the Santa Cruz Mountains as an area of potential super premium production, an area capable of producing world class wines.

Almaden's story in these years is complex and symbolic. Benoist, with the help of Schoonmaker, and for a while Alexis Lichine, raised the company's quality sights several notches during and after the war. More and better vines were planted and a 241 acre tract nearby was purchased for this purpose. All the while the stress was on good varietals and Champagne, although Almaden did have a full line of generic wines. Schoonmaker wrote an informative customer newsletter and designed a set of light hearted labels that are still used on many Almaden wines. The Grenache Rose caught on best with customers, but a bad fire and tight times after the war forced Benoist to merge for a short period with the huge Madrone Winery to the south. The Cribaris had sold this big wine factory to a group of businessmen in 1944 in order to concentrate their efforts on their Evergreen establishment.

The Madrone operation, with its 1,750,000 gallon capacity was to make generics. Almaden, now with 250,000 gallons of capacity, concentrated on varietals. This arrangement did not work well and after a year the two operations split. By 1952 Madrone had ceased operating and was later torn down after serving as an auto repair facility for several years. A huge water tower today marks where it once stood.

Meanwhile Benoist kept expanding and extending Almaden. He went outside the area to buy grapes he considered choice, such as the Digardis' great Gamay from the Martinez area. He also acquired vineyard land in the Livermore Valley and joined with Wente, Louis Martini and Korbel to expand and promote the eastern market for California premium wines. With Goulet at the winemaker's helm, a complicated sherry solera was developed. Almaden was one of the first in California to employ the German Willmes press to take the place of previous, rougher mechanisms.

Benoist was a real bon vivant, and part of the extended condition of Almaden was occasioned by his own personal extension and use of its resources. At one time, by the late 1960's he and his wife owned seven houses, two airplanes and a 110 foot yacht. A later industry study of Almaden concluded, perhaps too harshly, but not totally without accuracy, that Benoist's high life and "profligate spending" had hurt the company and placed it in a "precarious financial position."

Whatever his failings Benoist saw the proper course for Almaden's salvation and in 1954 started taking steps that would help insure its future.

In 1945 Otto Meyer joined Fromm and Sichel to take charge of the Paul Masson operations. By now there were about 100 acres of top varieties on La Cresta: Chardonnay, Pinot Noir, Gamay, Cabernet Sauvignon, Pinot Blanc and Folle Blanche. In the same year the new owners acquired the 1905 Monte Vista Winery near the old Villa Maria above Cupertino. This expansion greatly facilitated Champagne production. In 1946 the Masson label again appeared on the market.

Masson management also had to face up to slightly rising wine consumption and the decline of available vineyard land in the area. In 1956 they bought the 330 acre San Ysidro Ranch near Gilroy. It had been planted to good varietals in 1948. One of these was the Emerald Riesling, a variety developed at the University in 1939 and released in 1946. It became the basis for Masson's popular Emerald Dry. The company became more diversified in 1953 when the first brandy under the Masson label was released.

One of the finest modern wine structures in the Central Coast went up in Saratoga in 1959 when Masson completed their beautiful Champagne Cellars. It became a must-see for visitors to the valley. The facility also served as a finishing, bottling, packaging and shipping plant for the growing concern.

Now at the end of the decade, the Paul Masson company, like Almaden, had to reconcile rising wine consumption and growing sales with the dwindling vineyard area of the Santa Clara Valley.

In Evergreen the Mirassou Winery continued the pattern set during the war. Max Huebner by now was making really outstanding premium wines, which the family sold to other wineries, particularly Paul Masson. Huebner also developed a remarkable skill as a Champagne maker, employing a strict *methode Champenois*. He also experimented with a variety of styles and bases for his sparklers. For his own amusement he sometimes played with berry, orange juice, even coffee bases. Meanwhile Mirassou's wine could not be bought in any shop, but it did become available at the winery. Here Huebner would greet visitors, show them about and sell cases of the "vintner's dozen (thirteen bottles)." The varietals available included Cabernet Sauvignon, Gamay Beaujolais, Zinfandel and Semillon. Probably the Mirassous' best loved wine during these years was the Pinot Blanc. Nearby at the grand Wehner/Haentze place the Cribaris finally sold the vineyards to a land development company. Mirassou later contracted to use the great Wehner winery for storage.

In the south county San Martin was the leader after the war. The Filice family's approach was to be just about all things to all wine drinkers. They produced varietals, generics and a wide range of fruit wines and flavored wines. In 1954 they bought the California Wine Association's Guasti bulk Champagne making equipment and sold sparkling wine to other wineries who wanted some on their list but didn't have the facilities to make it. San Martin became best known in this area and to drivers between Northern and Southern California for its large wine tasting facility, built in 1958, at the winery on Highway 101. It was said that about 10% of the winery's production went through this tasting room. The Felices also expanded their vineyard holdings and increased the winery's capacity to about 2,000,000 gallons by 1960.

Perhaps even more important than the development of the larger industrial character of local winegrowing in these years was the renewal of the desire to make the region a producer of world class wines. There were a few who knew of Rixford, Klein and Pfeffer. Just as important was the American people's growing interest in high quality table wine, for there had to be a market that would support the extra intensity, care and expense inherent in the production of great wine.

Actually, a good part of that market had always been there. Before Prohibition those who were willing to pay the extra price for a bottle of Niebaum's Inglenook or Rixford's La Questa were never lacking. Now since Repeal a really keen interest in premium wines in the Bay Area and in Southern California was also becoming manifest. Soon after Repeal the British based International Wine & Food Society had a San Francisco chapter, others followed. The local Sauterne Club was not a phenomenon unique to the Santa Clara Valley. Soon there was a San Francisco based Medical Friends of Wine, which appealed to the

Emilio and Emilia Guglielmo immigrated in the 1900's to later establish their vineyard and winery near several Italian families in Morgan Hill. Neighbors and helpers are seen in the 1940's helping with the crush. Today, a third generation of Guglielmo's, George and Gene, continue the warmth and hospitality of this family run winery. (Gulglielmo Collection)

150

same kind of intense interest in fine wine as a part of civilized life. Writers such as Frank Schoonmaker, Tom Marvel and Robert Balzer drew attention to California's long history of premium wine. In 1958 Leon Adams added his *Commonsense Book of Wine,* which stripped away much of the irrelevant nonsense about wine that might intimidate beginners.

Before Prohibition those connoisseurs who had acquired a love for world class wine often had traveled in Europe and had seen at first hand the traditions of Bordeaux, Burgundy and the Rhine. But these were persons with means to cross the Atlantic in the glory days of the great steamship lines. These folks weren't really common and often their aristocratic ways were more a matter of scorn than emulation in this somewhat egalitarian republic. But after World War II millions returned from Europe and in the next years even more millions of tourists traveled rather freely and inexpensively to and from the continent. Here was a solid base of middle class folk who at least had been exposed to western European wine culture and the relationship of good wine and good food.

To this cultural development must be added the general improvement in California wines after World War II and the program to educate Americans in the value of good table wine. There was no way that the typical bottle of California wine of the 1930s could attract the interest of people who knew good European wine.

There was also more and more emphasis on the production of varietal wines and this really called for some education. It would soon be a matter of simple savvy not to think that Burgundy was the name of a grape or that Cabernet was a winegrowing area in France. Much of the quality boom in ordinary California wines derives from the scientific work at the University's Davis campus where the Department of Viticulture and Enology hammered away at techniques for producing better wine, if not necessarily world class wine. The main drive for this kind of development came primarily from idealists and fanatics inside and outside the academic world, intent on producing the best wine possible.

In this area the earliest drive for premium wines, after Repeal, came from the higher elevations. After his sale of Paul Masson to Seagram in 1943, Martin Ray did buy land to the north and planted the hilltops to Cabernet Sauvignon, Pinot Noir and Chardonnay vines. He was intent on making the greatest wine in North America by adhering strictly to the best traditional French winemaking techniques. The Cabernet vines Ray first planted came from cuttings taken from the

151

still very much alive Rixford vines in Woodside. He also worked on the old vines and put them back in order by pruning and training the gnarled oldtimers. From 1946 to 1948 Martin Ray Cabernets were made from these vines and have been praised as some of the greatest modern red wines ever made in California. The 1948 is still rich, tough and beautiful. These wines were made at the Gemello Winery in Mountain View. Later vintages up on the mountain were usually, but not always, successful and the chances that Ray took in producing his still wines and Champagne ocasionally had unfortunate results. But when they were good they were superior examples of the potential of the Chaine d'Or. There is more than one California wine maker today who traces his idealism and hopes to early tastes of Martin Ray wines. [15]

On the other side of the mountains, just above Felton, Chaffee Hall founded his Hallcrest Vineyard in 1941. He was a devoted wine lover and connoisseur who heeded the advice of those like Maynard Amerine who knew well the history of wine from the Bonny Doon and Ben Lomond area. Hall was a successful San Francisco lawyer who planted Hallcrest as a sort of retirement venture. He had the land cleared and planted about 13 acres of White Riesling and Cabernet Sauvignon. Hall has been quoted as saying, "I'd rather win a gold medal for my wines at the Sacramento Fair than a legal victory before the Supreme Court of the United States." [16] It was just this kind of idealistic enophilia that marked the efforts of Martin Ray and of others who followed these two in years to come. Both Hallcrest and Martin Ray took part in the formation of the Chateau Winegrowers Association in 1952, aimed at promoting such small scale, high quality operations. It did not take long for the small and growing body of Californians who wanted to taste the best from their state to make Hallcrest wines a special item of knowledgeable insidership.

There were a couple of other special premium operations started up in these years. Dan Wheeler began making wine in 1952 at his Santa Cruz Mountain home above Soquel. He too aimed at a natural process of winemaking that derived from a philosophy similar to Martin Ray's. Down in the valley Walter Richert, a man with a wide variety of credentials in the industry, opened a premium sweet wine operation next to the defunct Madrone Winery. Later he moved to the Paradise Valley Winery, long unused west of Morgan Hill. For years he produced some of the best sherries and ports in California.

The rise of quality in local wines can be gauged fairly accurately by the results at the State Fair competitions. It was a remarkable turnaround from the dismal days before World War II. At the 1947

Fair, Almaden and Novitiate showed that a new era had arrived. Almaden was tops for its Cabernet Sauvignon and Novitiate scored a first with their Black Muscat, a perennial favorite. Next year Almaden cleaned up with its whites. They won golds and silvers for Pinot Blanc, White Riesling, Semillon, Sylvaner and Traminer. Mirassou had its first success with a bronze for their White Riesling. 1950 and 1951 were Almaden years again. But Paul Masson had awards for their Pinot Noir and Gamay Beaujolais; Novitiate had a gold for Sauvignon Blanc and a silver for Zinfandel. The pattern was now pretty well set. The Santa Clara Valley and Santa Cruz Mountains were back in the premium game. In the years that followed the most important feature was Mirassou's coming of age. In 1958, for example, they won a White Riesling gold and a silver for Sylvaner. In 1954 a special gold medal went to Almaden for an experimental Duriff.

There were lots of medals handed out at Sacramento, perhaps a few too many. But in 1958 the prestigious *Consumer Reports* came out with a list of recommended California premium wines. There were 13 endorsements for Santa Clara County. Almaden, Paul Masson and Novitiate all received multiple recommendations. All three drew the nod for Cabernet Sauvignon and Semillon.

At the end of the decade there were a little fewer than 4,000 acres of vines in Santa Clara County, but they still represented about 10% of the wine grapes in the premium Coastal Counties. But the number of bonded wineries had dropped from 40 to 29, the dropouts mostly among the south county operations. But this category of country winery had become an extremely important factor in the local wine scene, as more and more consumers discovered in these friendly operations a very good source for dry table wine by the gallon. There were some that had gone under: Bouret, Athenour, Pourroy, Meyer and LaMalfa. Even the Villa Maria ceased operations when Santa Clara University sold off their 322 acres at the end of the war.

But there were some new country wineries selling their gallons at local retail stores and at the winery. Herman Mirassou's sons had revived the Lone Hill Winery after the war, an operation that lasted until it fell to subdivisions in 1968. Ed Gillick sold several varietals by the jug from his 1952 winery on Blossom Hill Road, just up the street from Almaden. In the south county the Pedrizzetti and Guglielmo Wineries developed fine reputations for their reds. Cassa Brothers in the Hecker Pass area became a regular stopping place for people who loved their slightly sweet Grenache Rose, which they styled "Rose Grape Wine." Bonesio, Bertero and Scagliotti continued their country

operations. The same function was performed on the Santa Cruz Mountain side by the Picchetti Winery on Montebello, the Locatelli Winery above Ben Lomond and the Bargetto Winery outside Soquel.

This flocking of local wine drinkers to these country wineries was symbolic of more than a change in tastes and drinking habits. The presence close at hand of these new wine buffs in large number was a sign of the suburban growth that transformed the Santa Clara Valley in the 1950s and that permanently changed the pattern of winemaking in the valley. Many valley vineyards had become obviously unproductive. Virus infection was common and nematodes in the soil cut back potential crops. North country vineyardists were loathe to replant as tract homes moved in on them. In the south county replanting was fairly common. But the best winegrowing land was still in areas not meant for residential tracts. These foothill and mountains lands would not fall so easily to the subdivider.

By the end of the decade the handwriting was on the wall and Louis Benoist appears to have been the first to have read it and to act. In 1955 Almaden leased the Valliant/Palmtag Winery in the Cienega Valley in San Benito County. This area had a long history of premium winegrowing dating back well into the 19th century. Edward Valliant had produced some of California's best white wines after Repeal. There were 507 acres of vines, some a half century old. There was also a fine old winery sitting astride the San Andreas fault, with a 675,000 gallon capacity. Next year Almaden was able to acquire the 2200 acre George Sykes Ranch at Paicines, to the east of Cienega and south of Hollister. These were planted to good varietals on their own roots, since the sandy soil of this area was not a happy environment for phylloxera.

Paul Masson was soon to follow, although their land purchase near Gilroy in 1956 stayed their move farther south for a few years. Eventually, in 1960 Masson bought 750 acres in the Salinas Valley near Soledad. This Monterey County purchase was but a start of the transfer of Masson's operations to the south. Mirassou also acquired land and planted vineyards in Monterey County during the 1960s. But they were able to maintain their large home vineyard in the face of advancing housing developments and also gained control of the vineyards that were left at the Wehner place and at Haentze's Villa Vista in Evergreen.

Thus it came to pass that the large winery operations of the Santa Clara Valley were forced south to insure a dependable grape supply to help satisfy America's growing thirst for good table wine. It is, however, noteworthy that each of these large companies has conscientiously maintained its Santa Clara Valley residence. It is doubtful that the only consideration was economic. The leaders of these wineries had come to understand that the industry was not running in place and that the roots of the second great California wine boom were firmly set.

Notes for Chapter VII

1. *Mercury*, 11/30/1932, 12/11/1932; Adams, Oral History, 53-54.
2. *Mercury*, 12/14/1933.
3. *Mercury*, 8/15/1930.
4. *W&V*, 9/1935.
5. *Mercury*, 4/8/1936.
6. Robert Lawrence Balzer, *The Pleasures of Wine* (New York, 1964), 145-6; Adams, 364; John Melville, *Guide to California Wines* (San Carlos, 1955), 121-2; Hinkle, 145; Garrod, 85, 143; *W&V*, 12/1940; San Jose *Evening News*, 7/8/1941.
7. *W&V*, 7/1937; *News*, 3/7/1979; Adams, 375; Hinkle, 135-7; Melville, 126-7.
8. *W&V*, 9/1941; *The American Wine Merchant*, 10/1942, hereafter *AWM*.
9. *AWM*, Spring, 1943; *W&V*, 1/1943. 11/1944.
10. Adams, 364-5; *W&V*, 4/1943; Balzer, 147.
11. *Evening News*, 5/1/1942, 11/13/1942; *AWM*, 12/1942.
12. *AWM*, Summer, 1943.
13. *W&V*, 12/1944; Adams, oral history, 86-8; Leon D. Adams, *The Commonsense Book of Wine* (New York, 1964), 19-21.
14. *W&V*, 11/1944, 2/1946, 2/1950, 10/1951; California History Center file, paper #1551; Adams, *Wines of America*, 372-3.
15. Janet Loustaunou, "A History of Woodside Wineries," *La Peninsula* (Summer, 1980), 4-5; Interview with Mario Gemello, April 1974.
16. Balzer, 160; *W&V*, 2/1952.

VIII. THE WINE REVOLUTION 1960 -1980

To grow grapes and produce wine in
these mountains, you have to be a lot more
dedicated than you would somewhere else.
Most of us do it because we love it.
— Ken. D. Burnap, 1979

What happened to the California wine industry during the next twenty years might be called the "second wine boom." In many ways it was similar to what had happened in the 1880s. But there were some important differences. In the 1880s the rise in demand for California wine did not take place because of any fundamental change in American drinking habits. Part of it was natural growth and part was France's woe. Continued growth after the first boom was based solidly on a change in the makeup of the American population, but not on a basic change in behavior. The millions of immigrants that made up the so-called "new" immigration between 1890 and 1910 came predominently from south and central Europe. They were used to drinking table wine with their meals and they wanted a sound and inexpensive beverage. What happened between 1960 and 1980 has been a revolution, mostly in Americans' tastes.

Naturally, there was a lot more wine drunk. Americans drank 192% more wine in 1980 than in 1960. And the statistics on the type of wine drunk have been more than totally reversed. Today sweet wines make up less than 15% of the wines Americans drink. It was not until 1967 that dry wines took a slight lead, and this lead has been growing every year.

There is another side to the revolution concerning table wines. In 1960 74% of the table wine drunk in the United States was red; in 1980 it amounted to only 26%. In other words, a vast majority of the new wine drinkers were taking to whites and roses. And it must be admitted that a large percentage of these new drinkers are simply using white wine in place of hard liquor. So far as local wine is concerned, however, this latter aspect of the revolution has not been so hard hitting, since the glass of white wine taken at American bars today

157

comes most likely from grapes grown in the Central Valley. But the explosion in premium consumption has also been most noticeable in the white wine category.

Local grapes today go almost entirely into the production of premium wines, a fact indicating that one casualty of the revolution has been the small country winery. Actually, most surviving country wineries, one way or another, have tried to join in the production of premium wines.

THE BIG ONES

In 1967 Louis Benoist sold Almaden to National Distillers, a large corporation that had previously owned wineries in California during the war. There were no wholesale changes in leadership or in direction after the sale. In fact, there was remarkable continuity after Benoist left. Growth and expansion was still the order of the day and by 1980 Almaden was the third largest wine company in the United States. So far as the production of premium wines is concerned Almaden ranked number one.

Naturally, the source of the company's grapes became even more concentrated to the south, but Charles Lefranc's old winery site was still the center of operations. A pretty 18 acre vineyard was maintained, mostly for aesthetic purposes and also as a historic reminder of the place where Thée and Lefranc set the roots of the valley's wine industry. The old cellar has been kept up, although the Lefranc home burned down in a tragic 1974 fire.

Much of the Almaden production of generics comes from grapes raised in the Central Valley, but the San Benito and Monterey vineyards produce the company's premiums. In recent years the company has been able to continue its focus on the production of excellent premium wines, under the Almaden label and under a new Charles Lefranc label, honoring the father of Santa Clara Valley's commercial wine industry.

Paul Masson's evolution has been along similar lines. Today this company ranks third in national production in premium wines. The old winery today acts mostly as a showplace and site of very popular concerts and stage productions, although it is still used some for sweet wine ageing. The vineyards on La Cresta have been worn by time, but are still producing. Congress Springs Winery and Sherrill Cellars have used grapes from La Cresta for wines under their labels. Down in the valley the elegant Champagne Cellars on Saratoga Road now act as administrative headquarters and continue to fulfill their production function. The Central Valley also provides grapes for Masson's generic wines, but premium operations are now centered in Monterey County in the huge Pinnacles Vineyard and Winery east of Soledad.

The Mirassou Winery remains a family operation, although it has grown to almost industrial proportions. This growth in the production of premium wines under the Mirassou label has been remarkable over the last twenty years. In 1960 sales at the winery amounted to about 1350 cases; today the winery at Evergreen has a capacity of 2,500,000 gallons, all of which is ticketed for sales under the company label. This transformation in production and marketing accelerated during the 1960s as Norbert's and Edmund's sons, the so-called "fifth generation," began to take more and more part in the business. Huebner continued for many years as winemaster, dying in 1979. Most of Mirassou's 1125 acres of vines are located in Monterey County, but the family maintains its Santa Clara Valley vineyards in Evergreen and continues to produce some wines under the valley appellation.

If continuity marks the growth of the wineries discussed above, remarkable change is the chief characteristic of the other large scale operation in the Santa Clara Valley. In 1973 the Filice family sold the San Martin Winery to Texas based Southdown Corporation, which resold it to the gigantic Norton Simon company in 1977. The Filices maintained their ownership in the family vineyards.

The result at San Martin has been a revolution in wine quality and an intense focus on changing the previous diverse and multi-faceted production pattern to one of a few top wines from the best grape varieties. To effect this change the San Martin plant has been modernized with particular emphasis on cool fermentation facilities and small oak cooperage. Winemaster Edmund Friedrich has been an outspoken industry leader in the production of delicately flavored, low alcohol wines at the the 3,000,000 gallon facility. San Martin now gets its grapes from all over the premium coastal area and continues to produce wines that occasionally bear the Santa Clara Valley appellation. Another distinctive feature of San Martin's approach has been its labels, which inform the consumer in precise detail the source and percentage of all grapes that went into the wine in that bottle. By no means a unique idea among smaller premium wineries, this practice has been a singular innovation for such a large operation.

The Novitiate's history and image might seem to belie its inclusion among the area's larger wine producers, but their 600 acres of vines and 725,000 gallons of capacity place the winery among the big ones. The growing popularity of dry table wines since 1960 has encouraged the Jesuits here to cut back on sweet wine production and make more table wine. Also, the economic facts of life have forced the Novitiate's managers to give up the cultivation of their vineyards in their hills behind Los Gatos.

Today most wines here are made from grapes grown in San Benito and Stanislaus counties. The ownership of fairly vast stretches of land above the Novitiate residence and in the hills above the Lexington Reservoir has caused some friction in recent years. There have been attempts by the town of Los Gatos to acquire parts of this land through condemnation, to preclude any type of eventual intensive development there. There have also been attempts by the Mid-Peninsula Regional Open Space District to acquire the lands where the old 1930 vineyards still produce grapes for other wineries. All this was still up in the air in 1981. But there is also serious talk at the Novitiate, more than rumors, that the winery itself would sold sometime soon.

The Turgeon and Lohr Winery is difficult to categorize. It is a partnership between two Saratoga businessmen, Bernard Turgeon and Jerome Lohr. But it is large and growing, up to 500,000 gallons capacity in 1981. The partners planted grapes near Greenfield in the Salinas Valley in 1971 but built their winery right near downtown San Jose in 1974, next to the site of the long defunct Fredericksburg Brewery. The wines produced here carry the "J. Lohr" brand name on the label and have developed a reputation for quality and elegance. Most grapes come from the winery's 280 acres in Monterey County, but they do buy from others when they feel the need. Wineries the size of Turgeon and Lohr with similar premium objectives have been fairly common during the years of the Wine Revolution. There have been at least a score started up in the North Bay counties. But in this area all the 100,000 gallon plus wineries, with two exceptions, stem from older operations. The exceptions are Turgeon and Lohr and Ridge Vineyards.

Not all attempts to take advantage of the Wine Revolution have met success in this area. The trials of the Filice family after its sale of San Martin Winery are a good example. Their plan was to develop a wide ranging wine operation with several functional levels. They purchased and refurbished the idle La Malfa Winery in Morgan Hill, right next to the new freeway. Here they intended to recreate the tasting room success they had had at San Martin. For working wineries they purchased the Gemello Winery as a source of first rate premiums, but kept the old production personnel. They also set up shop near

Acampo, north of Lodi, with the sizeable Montcalm wine facility to supply their generics. Between 1974 and 1976 the whole plan collapsed. The La Malfa place is now another San Martin tasting room. Gemello is back in the hands of the original owners and the Montcalm operation now produces Robert Mondavi's jug wines.[1]

There was another large scale takeover that failed in the south county. The Pedrizzeti Winery, founded by John Pedrizzetti in 1938, became one of the most popular country wineries in the area in the 1960s. The winery was operated by Ed and Phyllis Pedrizzetti for several years and was taken over by them in 1968. Their reputation for red table wines such as Barbera and Zinfandel was widespread. Between 1973 and 1974 the winery was sold to a group styling itself as Varietal Vintners. They also purchased the Bonesio Winery in the Hecker Pass area. But this venture fell through and both wineries went back into the hands of the original owners. Since then the Pedrizzettis have moved into the production of premium wines and have developed a national distribution along with an expanded capacity of 360,000 gallons.[2]

The Pedrizzettis' cross-town neighbor, the Guglielmo Winery, has had a recent development similar to theirs, but with some differences. This country winery also developed an excellent reputation for jugs of tasty red wines after World War II and in recent years has also made a few premiums under the Mt. Madonna label. But the "Emile's" brand Burgundy, named for Emilio Guglielmo, the winery's founder, was so popular that it continued to be an important aspect of production at the 450,000 gallon winery. Guglielmo wines have also been a favorite as house wines in Bay Area restaurants.

HECKER PASS

The greatest transformation in winegrowing has taken place in the Hecker Pass area west of Gilroy. In the years after World War II its numerous Italian winegrowers developed a district dotted with country wineries making mostly dry red table wine for local consumption. In the last twenty years a number of changes have been made.

Several of the wineries have taken up premium production. The Cassa Brothers Winery was bought by Ernest Fortino in 1970. Here, with the help of his brother Mario, he transformed the old jug operation into a 100,000 gallon winery whose red wines in a somewhat Italianate style have won a bag full of medals at the Los Angeles County Fair. Mario soon split off and built his own little winery next door. Today Ernest's Fortino Winery and Mario's Hecker Pass Winery control about 30 acres of vines and take part in a fairly intense rivalry that has produced numerous awards and many satisfied customers.

The Bonesio Winery also went into the production of numerous varietals under their "Uvas" label even before the Varietal Vintners contretemps. Louis Bonesio then sold the old winery in 1976 to Nikola Kirigin Chargin who had taken a degree in enology at Yugoslavia's University of Zagreb and later made wine at several California wineries. The winery's products now appear under the "Kirigin" label.

A few of the country places followed old patterns. Peter Scagliotti continued to greet visitors at his Live Oaks Winery tasting room and across the Hecker Pass Road the Bertero Winery built a new tasting room from which to sell their country wines. In 1981 the winery was sold to new owners. Nearby the Giretti and Conrotto Wineries no longer display a retail sign, but still sell to old customers. Conrotto's jug wines have recently found their way into at least one quality bottle shop on the San Francisco Peninsula.

Probably the most significant development in this area has been the founding of three new premium wineries. Thomas Kruse founded his little operation next to Bertero in 1971. Kruse has gained a good reputation for several of his varietals, but mostly smiles for his 1974 Thompson Seedless wine.

Across the road Marilyn Otteman founded her Sarah's Vineyard winery in 1978 and made her first wine that year from purchased grapes. The vineyard was planted in 1980 to high quality varietals that will test the Hecker Pass area's ability to produce premium white wines.

Nearby on Uvas Road Terry Parks founded his Sycamore Creek Vineyards in 1976. The winery is located on 16 acres formerly part of the old Solis Rancho. Seven acres are in old vineyard that once served the pre-Prohibition Marchetti Winery here. Parks' approach has been to make elegant wines of great intensity and strong varietal character.

There are also several very good older vineyards in the Hecker Pass and Uvas areas that have provided good red varieties, particularly Zinfandel and Petite Sirah, to local winemakers and to others outside the area.

NEW PATTERNS

It should be obvious from the previous discussion that today most of the wine made in the Santa Clara Valley and the Santa Cruz

Mountains is from grapes grown outside the area, mostly in Monterey, San Luis Obispo and Santa Barbara Counties. In Santa Clara County the land devoted to wine grapes amounted to about 1715 acres in 1980. This was now less that 2% of the vineyard area in the coastal counties. Santa Cruz County had but 100 acres in 1980, but it is important to remember that most of the vineyard land in the Santa Cruz Mountains is actually on the Santa Clara County side of the summit. Red varieties still predominated in Santa Clara County. So far as distribution was concerned, some 30% of these acres were located in the northern part of the county, in the mountains and foothills on the west side and around Evergreen. The rest were in the southern portion of the county, mostly south of Coyote.

The following lists of the leading varieties for the county speak fairly well for the quality potential, particularly for the red varieties. The chief varieties in the 100 acres in Santa Cruz County are: 1. Pinot Noir, 2. Chardonnay, 3. White Riesling, 4. Cabernet Sauvigon.

Wine Grape Acres, Santa Clara County, 1980[3]

Red Wine		White Wine	
Cabernet Sauvignon	217	French Colombard	98
Zinfandel	155	Pinot Blanc	72
Carignane	130	Semillon	70
Petite Sirah (Duriff)	101	Emerald Riesling	58
Pinot Noir	94	Chardonnay	50
Gamay Beaujolais	75	Chenin Blanc	38
Mataro	43	Malvasia Bianca	35
Ruby Cabernet	30	Palomino	31
Grignolino	30	White Riesling	31
Merlot	29	Sylvaner	26
Grenache	28	Muscat Blanc	25
Malvoisie (Cinsaut)	20	Green Hungarian	20

Another aspect of the new patterns in winegrowing here is the role of organization, both governmental and industrial. Organized government assistance aimed specifically at the wine grape grower has been a very positive element in the recent local picture. The most helping hand has come from the Cooperative Extension work of the University of California in conjunction with the U.S. Department of Agriculture. Beginning in 1969 this service initiated a series of timely, problem oriented pamphlets aimed directly at the area's winegrowers. Titled "Pressing Items," "Grape Squeezes," and "Grape Press," these publications together comprise a fine volume on the cultural and technical aspects of winegrowing here. Their author has been Farm

Advisor Rudy Neja, whose base of operation was San Jose until 1972, when his office followed the expansion of grape plantings to the south and was relocated in Salinas.[4]

The industry itself has also formed several organizations to promote local wines and to share information and social amenities. The "greater" Santa Clara County group is the largest, but the south county has a group of its own. The Santa Cruz Mountain organization is probably the most tightly knit and intensely functional. A very large part of the growing complexity of the local wine scene derives from the activities of these industry organizations. Tastings, festivals, picnics, concerts, seminars, T-shirts and the promotion of historical research have all resulted from their efforts.

Another very obvious feature of the new times is the growing equality of the sexes in the local industry, a phenomenon fairly general in the industry as a whole. Women are taking far more than the sometimes symbolic equal partnership in many of the smaller wineries. Jan Sherrill, Valerie Ahlgren, Robin Gehrs and Marjorie Staiger are obvious examples from the Santa Cruz Mountains. In larger corporate operations women are now found in all manner of positions virtually closed to them twenty years ago. Some manage the winemaking itself. Meredith Edwards was the winemaker at Mt. Eden for several vintages. Marilyn Otteman is in charge of the cellar at Sarah's Vineyard. In 1977 Phyllis Pedrizzetti was elected president of the Santa Clara County Winegrowers Association as was Beverly Oaks in 1981. She is the assistant to Almaden's winemaster.

Medals may not prove that a wine is the best there is, but they obviously attest to the willingness of the winemaker to compete with others. Such a confidence was almost totally lacking after Repeal and somewhat tentative in later years in this area. The results in the last few years might actually make some local winemakers somewhat cocky. Two leading competitions supply fairly convincing data.

In 1979 at the Los Angeles County Fair twenty local wineries won 52 medals, or 13% of all awards. Ahlgren, Fortino, Turgeon & Lohr, Pedrizzetti, Staiger, Roudon-Smith, Bargetto, San Martin and Mirassou all won gold medals. The Novitiate won seven silver medals. These statistics were compiled without the entry of several of the most important local wineries, whose absence was certainly not due to any lack of quality in their products. In 1980 11% of the awards went to locals, with Page Mill and Novitiate adding their names to the gold medal list. At the 1980 Orange County Fair, where wines are rated in categories of price and chemical composition, local wineries won 9% of the awards, with golds going to Almaden, Ridge, Smothers, Felton-Empire and Fortino.

One of the factors that has increased the zeal for quality has been the recent home winemaking craze. Several of the wineries mentioned above started out as vinous hobbies. For some years on the San Francisco Peninsula a home winemakers group met and exchanged notes. Its acronym was PHEW! for Peninsula Home Enology Workshop. There are probably more high quality home vineyards per capita here in the hills around Interstate 280 than any comparably sized area in North America.

Selling grapes to home winemakers has actually become a fairly important aspect of local viticulture. These fanatics will pay top dollar for the right grapes. One group of home winemakers in the Almaden Valley has purchased Zinfandel grapes from every vineyard in that area to produce a whole line of quality wines for their own pleasure. In the Hecker Pass area John Roffinella acts as a wine grape broker for home enthusiasts. In the Saratoga area there are numerous small vineyards that sell to home winemakers and to local wineries.

APPELLATION SANTA CRUZ MOUNTAINS

In 1980 the winegrowers of the Santa Cruz Mountains applied to the U.S. Treasury Department for their own appellation of origin. When approved, wine made from grapes within this delineated zone might carry the appellation on its label. At the subsequent hearings conducted in the city of Santa Clara numerous witnesses testified to the special excellence of the area's mountain wines. It was argued that grape for grape and bottle for bottle it was the top viticultural district in California. It would be difficult to argue otherwise. There are no ordinary grapes planted any place in these mountains, save a couple of acres of Sauvignon Vert near Lexington. There are no jug wines, no winemakers with any kind of casual attitude toward their vocation. There were only about 250 acres of these choice grapes here in 1980, but there are many who have started making plans to bring the area's acreage up to levels it enjoyed around the turn of the century. This would call for a 600% increase, which, given the enthusiasm and devotion to the mountains' special soil and climate, seems somewhat tame in the long run.

❧ ❧ ❧ · ❧ ❧ ❧ ❧ ❧

Following Martin Ray's brief use of the old Rixford vineyards at Woodside during the 1940s, the area was gradually subdivided. Robert Groetzinger, one of the new residents, discovered the La Questa vines and in 1957 made wine from them, training some up and cutting back the jungle that had developed in the previous decade. He got together with another local, Robert Mullen, the result being that several pieces of the old La Questa vineyard resting on the one acre lots of residents on the hill have been resuscitated and augmented. Mullen founded Woodside Vineyards in 1963 and began producing Cabernet Sauvignon under a revived La Questa label. He "ranches" the four remaining plots of Cabernet and buys from others in the area. On his own piece of land nearby, on Kings Mountain Road, he raises Chardonnay and Pinot Noir. And like others, he has bought outside the area to augment the limited supply of local mountain grapes. Until 1973 Mullen's little winery under the carport was the smallest bonded operation in California.

Others followed. Nathaniel and Jan Sherrill started as home winemakers and in 1972 established their little bonded winery in the cellar of the Woodside Post Office. In 1978 they built a little winery a bit to the south and higher up, near Skyline Boulevard. The Sherrills have gone far afield to acquire grapes for their powerful wines, mostly red. But they have begun a small Chardonnay vineyard at the new place.

The Sherrill partnership illustrates a very significant aspect of the Wine Revolution in the Santa Cruz Mountains. He is an electrical engineer; she is a writer and university counselor. The closeness of concentrated electronics industry and academia in the valley makes it possible for professionals to continue their daily work and retreat to the mountains and foothills to invest their human capital in their wine operations. In this way there is a steady income and ability to concentrate on quality without desperate concern for profits. No great fortunes are being made by Santa Cruz Mountains winegrowers, at least not yet. No fewer than seventeen of the new mountain ownerships since 1960 derive from this kind of situation. There are physicians, pilots, engineers and educators. The electronics industry of "Silicon Valley" has contributed a large portion of these participants in the Revolution.

Another San Mateo winery is located near Half Moon Bay, not a good place to raise wine grapes. Paul and Sandy Obester buy their grapes from many sources, from Mendocino to Monterey, their first crush coming in 1977. Sandy's grandfather was John Gemello who helped out during the first two crushes. Another small winery is located well to the south, on the Santa Clara County side, the Page Mill Winery. Richard Stark was another home winemaking, electronics man who decided to try his hand at the commercial game. His 1978 Cabernet Sauvignon won a gold medal at Los Angeles.

If ever the government begins to grant sub-appellations, Montebello/Mt. Eden should have one of the first calls on a special district label. The recently planted vineyards here on the higher elevations have strangely mixed viticultural personalities, for to date the greatest triumphs have come from Chardonnay and Cabernet Sauvignon, vines that traditionally enjoy somewhat dissimilar environments.

At the top of Montebello Ridge Dr. Perrone's nephew died in 1943, but the old vineyards had long since expired. In 1949 William Short bought part of the old estate and began replanting. Short was a doctor of theology who had been jailed during World War I for having opposed the draft. He was a man of many parts, as was his successor on the Ridge, David R. Bennion, who, with several associates at Stanford Research Institute, bought the place in 1960 and began making wine. During the next twenty years Ridge wines became totally identified with all the best aspects of the premium side of the Wine Revolution. From the outset Bennion focused on many of Martin Ray's goals: intensity, natural processes, varietal definition, ageing potential. And like Ray some of his early efforts stumbled. But the vast majority were intense, concentrated and long lived. To drink a bottle of 1968 Ridge Montebello Cabernet Sauvignon in 1978 was to commit vinocide.

During the early years the wines were made at an old farm building on the property. Zinfandel grapes were purchased from the Picchettis and more were planted on top, particularly Cabernet Sauvignon. Later operations were moved up to the main Perrone Winery and expanded to a capacity of 150,000 gallons. Bennion had wanted to label his early wines Montebello Ridge, but the first term was still owned by the successor company that Dr. Perrone had helped set up a half century before. Thus Ridge became the name on the label for a wide variety of wines made from grapes grown all over the northen and central part of the state. There were even good wines made from Lodi Zinfandels. Downhill, at the old Pierre Klein place, the Schwabacher family was encouraged to plant the old terraces to wine grapes. Today this Jimsomare Vineyard is an important source for many of the grapes going into wines labeled "Montebello" as a source, if not a brand. There are about 75 acres of vines on Montebello Ridge, making this area the largest in vine concentration in the Santa Cruz Mountains. But there are some on the other side of the mountains who think this distinction can't last many more years.

At no place in California winemaking has the ferment of the Wine Revolution been more lively and controversial than on Table Mountain, to the south of the Ridge, where Martin Ray set up his vineyards and winery after his sale of the Paul Masson Company in

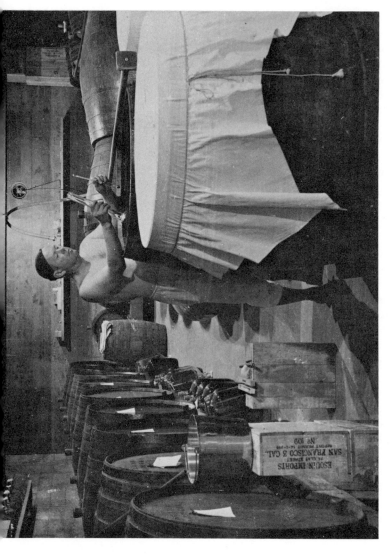

Martin Ray at fermentation tanks checks progress of wine with hydrometer. This personal attention to winemaking produced world class wines in the chaine d'or. (*Martin Ray Collection*)

1943. During the 1950s Martin Ray developed a reputation for great wines sold at absolutely astronomical prices. He also developed a highly unflattering personal image in the wine industry, an image in which he took great pride. He was thoroughly convinced that he was the only person in California making really great wine in the old French tradition. As one writer put it, he sent down "reams of bombastic literature" from his mountain height. "It stings because it has barbs of truth. It offends because of its boasting." Ray lashed out continuously at loose government regulations that allowed wines to have no more than 51% of the indicated varietal. He was particularly incensed by the use of grape concentrates by even the most respected wineries. He demanded that appellations of origin be established and enforced. He gave and asked no quarter and developed a dedicated following and a long list of persons who despised him.

In 1959 he stated that "California winegrowing must have new people with culture and ideals." To help effect this goal he brought together about 25 wealthy wine devotees and with their capital he expanded the vineyards to over twenty acres. But his relations with this Mt. Eden group, mostly California physicians, soon deteriorated. The result was a decade of conflict that ended in an ugly court battle and a sheriff's sale in 1971. The assets of the Martin Ray Domaine were divided so that Ray kept only his home and the five acre Chardonnay vineyard in front of it. The battle continued and grew even more bitter, with his own little winery locked up by legal order during the 1975 vintage. When Martin Ray died in 1976, there were few who, at this date, would not pay him the encomiums due him. For practically everything he had fought for had come to pass or was in the process. As one national wine journal put it, "He was feared and hated by many people, but in his eccentric way he was the catalyst for the entire wine industry, and showed others what could be accomplished if they thought big and never compromised."[6]

The next half decade at the Martin Ray Winery has been much calmer but no less devoted to making fine wines. Peter Ray, Martin Ray's adopted stepson, has taken charge of the little winery. This was no rough transition, since he had been supervising much of the winemaking since 1958. His vocation as professor of plant physiology at Stanford University indicates a scientific background quite useful to the serious winegrower.

Some of the wine produced under the Martin Ray label today comes from grapes grown outside the Santa Cruz Mountains. But there is a continuing devotion on the part of the new leaders of the revived winery to the use of Santa Cruz Mountain grapes whenever they can be had.[7]

The 23 acres of the Martin Ray Domain that the Mt. Eden Group finally acquired in 1971 now produces wine under the Mt. Eden label. The wines made here since 1972 have been no less intense and long lived than when Martin Ray controlled the vineyards. And the internal strife and factionalism among the physician owners has continued apace. There has been a rapid turnover of winemakers and in 1981 it was announced that the winery was for sale. Meanwhile more wine has been produced here by going outside the area for grapes and bottling the result under the MEV label.

If Mt. Eden were ever to become a sub-appellation of the Santa Cruz Mountains, there are several excellent private vineyards, mostly in Cabernet Sauvignon, that could supply grapes in the district. These are located off Mt. Eden and Pierce Roads and have supplied grapes for excellent Cabernets from the Gemello and Roudon-Smith Wineries in recent years. The grapes from the new Garrod vineyard, across the road from where E.H. Guppy started commercial winemaking almost a century ago, are going to Martin Ray.

Unlike other parts of the Chaine d'Or, the Congress Springs district has not come alive with vineyards since 1960. But the old Pourroy Winery, Monmartre, has been brought back to life and some of the old vineyards revived, some replanted, by Daniel Gehrs, his wife Robin and brother James. Gehrs went into production in 1976 with the financial backing of San Jose businessman Victor Erickson. Today Congress Springs Vineyards makes wine from its own 12 acres at the winery, from Masson's nearby La Cresta and from Novitiate's vineyards above Lexington. No winery in the mountains is more devoted to the unique possibilities of wines made from Santa Cruz Mountain grapes, a fact attested to by the Gehrs' almost exclusive use of local grapes.

❧ ❧ ❧ ❧ ❧ ❧ ❧ ❧

Except for the Novitiate vineyards planted in the 1930s, the important wine district between Lexington and the Summit and on the slopes of Loma Prieta has never been revived. Nearby, however, on Bear Creek Road, David Bruce established one of the first new wineries of the current Revolution. He acquired his property in 1961 and has since built a fine home and winery and planted 25 acres of vines on the surrounding hills, Chardonnay, Pinot Noir, Cabernet Sauvignon and White Riesling. Bruce is a graduate of Stanford

171

Medical School and continues his practice in the valley on a part time basis. He frankly admits to the influence of Martin Ray on his philosophy of winemaking, and like Ray has made great, intensely flavored and often controversial wines. Like Martin Ray his somewhat chancy, natural approach to winemaking has produced some failures. But Dr. Bruce has been flexible in adopting technological improvements where they do not conflict with the natural development of the powerful wines he personally loves. Like so many on the Santa Cruz side of the Summit, David Bruce's vinous ideal is Burgundian.

Farther down from the Summit toward Monterey Bay, winegrowing in the old Vine Hill district has been revived and in recent years two wineries have been established near where the Jarvis Brothers proved the premium character of the area over a century ago. The vineyard off Vine Hill Road has passed through several hands since the 1960s. Richard Smothers, previously well known in the entertainment world, bought it from Ridge Vineyards and made the vineyard and little winery something of an extension of the Felton-Empire Winery until 1979. James Beauregard managed the vineyard and Leo McCloskey made wine in 1977 and 1978, both of these men from the Felton operation. In recent years the wines made from the 14 acres of Chardonnay, White Riesling and Sylvaner have reaffirmed Vine Hill's quality potential.

Nearby on Rider Ridge, also in the Vine Hill district, close to the original Jarvis Winery, Ken Burnap has set up his Santa Cruz Mountain Vineyard and winery. Like David Bruce, Burnap aspires to make great wine in the Burgundian style. He bought 14 acres of Pinot Noir in 1974 and bonded his winery in 1975.

Burnap has been a constant critic of those who have planted too much of this grape in areas obviously unsuited for it. He is one of the leading spokesmen for the unique character of the Santa Cruz Mountain appellation and has long advocated expansion of vineyard planting here. He has added some Chardonnay to his plantings and made a remarkable Cabernet Sauvignon in 1978 from nearby mountain grapes. He has also made a wine he correctly labeled Duriff from grapes traditionally termed Petite Sirah in California. The government could not complain, since Duriff is the correct name of the grape.

Even closer to the Monterey Bay, and technically outside the Santa Cruz appellation, is the Bargetto Winery at Soquel, which had functioned much like many country wineries before the 1960s. When

Ralph and Lawrence Bargetto took over from their father in 1964 a gradual change of focus took place. There is still country wine in larger containers, and fruit and berry wines, but there have also been wines to match many of the best from the Santa Cruz Mountains. Bargetto buys grapes from the mountains, when possible, but like most in the area, buys elsewhere. There have been outstanding Chardonnays from Vine Hill and excellent White Rieslings from Santa Barbara.

Finally we come to the winegrowing district in the hills and foothills northwest of Scotts Valley and up the San Lorenzo River, the center of winegrowing in Santa Cruz County at the turn of the century: Felton, Ben Lomond, Bonny Doon and Boulder Creek. Here was Frona Wait's proclaimed "Chablis District" of 1889. There are several wineries in the area today, but few vineyards as yet. But the passion is there and it can be safely predicted that in the decade of the 1980s there will be more new vines planted here than were to be found in the entire county in 1979. For the time, however, most wineries here must go outside the area for grapes.

Close to where Dr. John Stewart raised his fine Cabernets in the 1890s is the Roudon-Smith Winery which had its first crush in 1972. A new winery was built in 1978 with grapes coming from several places outside the area and from local mountain vineyards. Near Felton the old Hallcrest Winery was leased in 1976 by a trio of wine enthusiasts who use the Hallcrest Cabernet and White Riesling and grapes from nearby vineyards. Winemaker Leo McCloskey has also worked in the lab at Ridge Vineyards since 1971, while viticulturist James Beauregard has an excellent vineyard near Bonny Doon. He is one of the chief movers in the area advocating the expansion of local vineyard plantings. The Felton-Empire Winery has made several remarkable wines since its founding in 1976, with a special emphasis on White Riesling in a very Germanic style.[9]

Above Ben Lomond the Vincent Locatelli Winery survived the post-Repeal years and produced wine under the Eagle Rock label through the 1950s. In 1976 biochemist Keith Hohlfeldt and several associates leased the old home and winery and began making wine under the Sunrise label. In the tradition of the Santa Cruz Mountains, the winery burned down in 1978. The result, however, indicates something of the spirit among the mountains' winegrowers in this new era. Almost to a man and woman they pitched in to restore the winery and pull the new operation through. Sunrise has used grapes from many areas but has placed special emphasis on the production of wines from local grapes. Cabernet Sauvignon from the Arata Vineyard of Saratoga has been particularly successful.

Closer to Boulder Creek the Ahlgren and Staiger Wineries have also added to the number attracted to this beautiful environment for winemaking. Dexter and Valerie Ahlgren's first crush was in 1976. Paul and Marjorie Staiger bonded their winery in 1973 and market their wines under the P. and M. Staiger label.

❦ ❦ ❦ ❦ ❦ ❦ ❦ ❦

The future of quality winegrowing in the Santa Cruz Mountains in the 1980s and 1990s appears remarkably propitious. The patterns established in the 1880s seem to indicate that fairly large scale commercial success and the production of good standard wines could be the area's lot. But the patterns established since the 1960s seem to indicate an intensive development that rests squarely on the efforts of idealistic individuals whose chief source of capital is themselves. Lots of ordinary grapes were planted in these mountains a hundred years ago. There is little possibility for such a development in the years to come.

The Santa Clara Valley will continue to be a winegrowing area, but vineyard acreage is destined to decline. The marvelous land than once seemed to explode into modern Edens over a century ago is now paved over or will be soon. Where viticulture and winemaking will survive is on the less rich soils on higher ground that are not inviting to the developer or subdivider. The great capital investment of the larger industrial wine operations in the valley seems to guarantee a continued presence for these historic wineries for years to come, even if the land nearby bears little fruit.

Looking at what has come down to us from the pioneer days of winegrowing in the Santa Clara Valley and Santa Cruz Mountains, we must own that the greatest part of what is left is now memory and a tradition, cherished by many but manipulated by some. The importance of this area to the development of the state's wine industry has been obvious, from the very earliest days to Prohibition. The great decline thereafter has been followed by a reawakening of the earliest pioneer ideals and inklings of a very important future.

The weaknesses in our pioneer roots are also apparent. The most serious of these must be traced to too strong a sense of individual attainment and too little sense of local pride and commitment to a community of winegrowers. There was too little concern for the developemnt of a wine personality for this area. The opposite was true in the North Bay and at least part of the difference in the two areas' wine history and long term success must be traced to this situation.

The gardens that our pioneer vineyardists created were "like modern Edens," as John Quincy Adams Warren marveled in 1863. There was better money to be made in surer crops. What does it take to sow grain, plant vegetables or herd livestock? Much, but nothing so much as is required of the person who sets out to be a vineyardist or orchardist. He must look long years into the future, and he must have vision. He must be patient, and when he is not, as was the case with many greenhorn winemen here, he pays dearly.

While others in the Santa Clara Valley and the surrounding mountains planted grain and herded cattle, these few pioneers, intelligent men, looked at the soil, marked the climate and understood that this area was meant for something more than wheat and livestock. They were correct. Fruit was to be the agricultural glory of the area. And until houses took over so much of the land, wine grapes were a very important part of the fruit crop. There are still many vines, the best on the elevated spots where it is less easy to plant a housing tract and where the worst farmland can be the proper home of a fine vineyard.

The physical remains from over a century ago are almost non-existent. Those from the Wine Boom of the 1880s are more common. Many of Emmett Rixford's vines still produce Cabernet Sauvignon grapes on LaQuesta. Some old wineries survive. The Picchetti place is now part of a regional park. The Perrone Winery still stands and functions. The Baldwin Winery is a college book store. Almost nothing survives from the early days in the Santa Cruz County. But Jarvis's tunnels along Branciforte Creek can still be seen by the interested history buff.

Little remains in the south Santa Clara Valley. But the old Malaguerra Winery near Morgan Hill is being developed into a historical wine museum by the Friends of the Winemakers, a local group founded by Novitiate's Brother Norbert Korte.

There is nothing much left of the East Side save the Wehner estate and its old home and winery. In San Jose virtually nothing survives. Delmas, Prevost and Naglee are recalled by the streets named for them. And recently a tiny park was dedicated to commemorate the contributions of the Pellier brothers.

Where the industry began, near Lone Hill and Guadalupe Creek, there are a few reminders of the past. David Harwood's Lone Hill Winery and its successors are long gone, but one of the palm trees marking the entrance on Harwood Road survives. The little hill itself has been quarried down so that few would realize that this spot was once a prominent geographic feature of the valley.

The place where commercial winegrowing began is still planted to vines by the current owners of Almaden Vineyards on Blossom Hill Road. Charles Lefranc's old cellar survives as do many of the gnarled pepper trees he planted on the estate. Guadalupe Creek still rushes from the hills above and courses its path through ancient sycamores behind the winery buildings. And to this day along its banks still grow and ripen the wild *Vitis californica* vines which vouchsafed to earliest pioneers an important clue about the valley's future.

Notes for Chapter VIII

1. *W&V*, 10/1974, 10/1975, 12/1976; *Wine World*, 5/1976.
2. *W&V*, 12/1973, 3/1974.
3. Santa Clara County Agricultural Commissioner's Report, 1980; cf. California Crop and Livestock Reporting Service, "California Grape Acreage, 1980." These sets of data vary to a great extent for some varieties. The statistics given are figures arrived at by the author from government data, personal observations and interviews.
4. These publications may be seen at 118 Wilgart Way, Salinas 93901.
5. San Francisco *Chronicle*, 6/24/1976; *Mercury*, 10/14/1979; San Francisco *Examiner*, 11/30/1980; Charles l. Sullivan, "More Women Making the Wine Scene," *Wine Spectator*, 4/1/1980.
6. Hinkle, 145; Adams, 366; Los Angeles *Times*, 1/26/1975; Los Angeles *Examiner*, 4/27/1969; Chicago *Tribune*, 3/18/1976; Robert W. Benson, "Martin Ray: Enfant Terrible of American Winemaking," *American Bar Association Journal*, (August, 1976), 1047-48; *Vintage*, 8/81, 19-22.
7. Saratoga *News*, 1/5/1980.
8. *News*, 5/3/1968; *Mercury*, 11/23/1975; *Wine World* (July-August, 1981), 30-31.
9. Mike Holland, "The Bonny Doon Grape War," *Santa Cruz Weekly*, March 11, 1981.

Large scale planting and expansion of production in the 1970's required improved technology. Mirassou was in the forefront of encouraging improved technology by working with University of California and Food Machinery engineers for the design of a mechanical harvester. *(Mirassou Collection)*

Ken Burnap in the barrel room of his Santa Cruz Mountain Vineyard Winery near where the famed Jarvis wines were made in the 1870s, close to Vine Hill. His 1977 Pinot Noir is recognized as one of the greatest modern achievements of California winemaking.

Ace Perry, Saratoga wine merchant dumping a box of grapes into the crusher at Martin Ray, in 1977, just after Martin's death. *(Martin Ray Collection)*

RIDGE
SANTA CRUZ MTNS
ZINFANDEL
MONTE BELLO
1979

79 Zinfandel, Monte Bello, bottled May 1981

In this vintage on Monte Bello Ridge, the old vines at the Picchetti Ranch and a part of those at the Jimsomare Ranch produced an elegant wine typical of the lighter years of the 1970s. After a full malo-lactic fermentation it was lightly fined and with barrel aging developed the distinctive varietal character unique to these vineyards. Despite firm acidity, this lovely wine should begin to soften by fall and develop further with two or three years of bottle age. PD (5/81)

Begun in 1959, Ridge was one of the first of today's chateau-size California wineries, that is, those that limit production in order to attempt the highest quality. All our wines are aged in small oak cooperage with the majority receiving no cellar treatment other than racking. Located above 2300 feet on Monte Bello Ridge in the Santa Cruz Mountains, we overlook San Francisco Bay. For information on ordering wines or visiting us for tasting, please send a note or call (408) 867-3233.   DRB (1/80)

NET CONTENTS

PRODUCT OF CALIFORNIA, U.S.A. 750ML

60% PICCHETTI VINEYARD & 40% JIMSOMARE VINEYARD
SANTA CRUZ MOUNTAINS   ALCOHOL 12.0% BY VOLUME
PRODUCED AND BOTTLED BY RIDGE VINEYARDS, BW4488
17100 MONTE BELLO ROAD, P.O. BOX A-1, CUPERTINO, CALIFORNIA

Paul Draper (PD) winemaker at Ridge since 1970 and David Bennion (DRB) one of the founders, now president of the winery, provide a few notes on the label of their historic Montebello Zinfandel. The spirit of Largo on a line at Ridge is reflected in

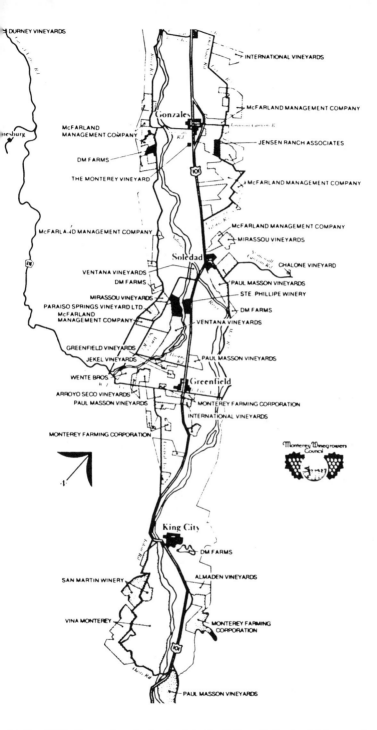

In the 1970's the exodus of wineries into the Salinas Valley is vividly seen in this Monterey Winegrowers Council map. Acreage of Santa Clara Valley wineries in Salinas Valley (1982) included: Mirassou 740 acres, Turgeon and Lohr 300 acres, Almaden 2,100 acres, Paul Masson 4,200 acres.

181

Sources

The chapter notes serve as a bibliography for this study. What follows is a list of works which deal directly with the history of the wine industry in Santa Clara Valley and the Santa Cruz Mountains. This is by no means a complete list and has been selected as a guide for the reader wishing to pursue this subject. The hundreds of articles in periodicals and newspapers on individual current wineries are not included.

Adams, Leon D. *The Wines of America*, New York, 1978, 2nd Edition.

Balzer, Robert Lawrence. *California's Best Wines*, Los Angeles, 1948.

_____ .*The Pleasures of Wine*, New York, 1964.

_____ .*This Uncommon Heritage: The Paul Masson Story*, Los Angeles, 1970.

Bancroft, Hubert Howe. *History of California*, 7 Vols., San Francisco, 1886.

Biggs, Donald C. *Conquer and Colonize*, San Rafael, 1979. Very useful for the life of Henry Naglee.

Butler, Phyllis Filiberti. *The Valley of Santa Clara*, San Jose, 1975. Good for old winery remains.

California History Center, De Anza College, Cupertino. *Cupertino Chronicle*, 1975.

Clemens, Scott. "Wineries of the Santa Cruz Mountains," *Vintage*, (July, 1979), 38-42; (August, 1979), 30-35.

Cook, Fred S. (ed.) *The Wines and Wineries of California*, Jackson, California, n.d. (ca. 1970)

Couchman, Robert. *The Sunsweet Story*, San Jose, 1967. Good on the Pelliers and local agriculture.

Cunningham, Florence R. *Saratoga's First Hundred Years*, Fresno, 1967.

Fischler, Susan. "Wine, Women and Naglee," Pioneer essay collection, California Room, San Jose Public Library, 1977.

Foote, H.S. *Pen Pictures from the Garden of the World*, Chicago, 1888.

Fox, Frances L. *Land Grant to Landmark*, San Jose, 1978. Information on Pierre Sainsevain.

Garrod, R.V. *Saratoga Story*, Saratoga, 1962.

Gates, Paul W. *California Ranchos and Farms, 1846-1862*, Madison, Wisconsin, 1967.

Hall, Frederic. *The History of San Jose*, San Francisco, 1871.

Hardy, Thomas. *Notes on the Vineyards in America and Europe*, Australia, 1885. Portions of this rare book were reprinted in *Wines & Vines*, September, 1966, *passim*. Good on Henry Naglee.

Hathaway, Susan. "Discovering the Vintage Valley," *California Today*, May 6, 1979.

_____."Santa Cruz Mountain High," San Jose *Mercury*, 10/14/1979.

Hinkle, Richard Paul. *Central Coast Wine Tour*, St. Helena, 1977.

Holland, Mike. "The Bonny Doon Grape War," *Santa Cruz Weekly*, 3/11/1981.

Hyatt, Thomas Hart. *Hyatt's Hand-Book of Grape Culture*, San Francisco, 1876.

Jacobs, Julius L. "California's Pioneer Wine Families, " *California Historical Quarterly*, (Summer, 1975), 139-174. For Pelliers and Mirassous.

Jones, Idwal. *Vines in the Sun*, New York, 1949. Loaded with interesting historical information; but often reads like historical fiction.

Kinnaird, Lawrence. *History of the Greater San Francisco Bay Region*, San Francisco, 1966.

Leggett, Herbert B. "Early History of Wine Production in California," Unpublished master's thesis, University of California, Berkeley, 1941.

Lewis, Jason Brandt. "A Look at the Santa Cruz Mountains," *Wine World*, (May, 1981), 30-36; (July, 1981), 30-35.

Loustaunou, Janet. "A History of Woodside Wineries," *La Peninsula*, (Summer, 1980.)

McKee, Irving. "Historic Wine Growers of Santa Clara County," *California — Magazine of the Pacific*, September, 1950.

_____."Jean Louis Vignes," *Wine Review*, July, 1948.

McKevitt, Gerald. *The University of Santa Clara*, Stanford, 1979.

Mars, Amaury. *Reminiscences of Santa Clara Valley and San Jose*, San Jose, 1901, reprinted, 1976.

Martin, Edward. *History of Santa Cruz County*, Los Angeles, 1911.

Melville, John. *Guide to California Wines*, San Carlos, California, 1955.

Morgan, Jefferson. *Adventures in the Wine Country*, San Francisco, 1971.

Munro-Fraser, J.P. *The History of Santa Clara County, California*, San Francisco, 1881.

Nasatir, Abraham P. *French Activities in California*, Stanford, 1945.

_____.*A French Journalist in the California Gold Rush*, Georgetown, California, 1964.

Payne, Stephen. *A Howling Wilderness*, California History Center, De Anza College, Cupertino, California, 1978. The families of the Santa Cruz Mountains.

Peninou, Ernest P. and Sidney S. Greenleaf. *A Directory of Wine Growers and Wine makers in 1860*, Berkeley, 1967.

Quakenbush, Margery (ed.) *County Chronicles*, California History Center, De Anza College, Cupertino, n.d.

Raymond, I.H. *Santa Cruz County*, Santa Cruz, 1877.

Reeve, Lloyd and Alice. *Gift of the Grape*, San Francisco, 1959.

Richards, Gilbert. *Crossroads*, Woodside, California, 1973. San Mateo County history.

Rixford, E.H. *The Wine Press and the Cellar*, San Francisco, 1883.

San Jose *Mercury. Santa Clara County and Its Resources*, San Jose, 1895. Reprinted as *Sunshine, Fruit and Flowers* by the San Jose Historical Museum, 1975.

Sawyer, Eugene T. *History of Santa Clara County*, Los Angeles, 1922.

Schoonmaker, Frank and Tom Marvel. *American Wines*, New York, 1941.

Sepeda, Dolores. *Hills West of El Toro*. Privately printed, 1978.

Sewill, Lynn M. "The Effect of Prohibition on the People of Santa Clara County," Pioneer Essay Collection, California Room, San Jose Public Library, 1977.

Stewart, Reginald R. *The Burrell Letters*, Oakland, 1960. Pioneer days in the Santa Cruz Mountains.

Sullivan, Charles L. "The Day They Robbed Paul Masson," *Vintage*, (July, 1979), 20-28.

_____."An Historian's Account of Zinfandel in California," *Wines & Vines*, (February, 1977), 18-20.

_____."Like Modern Edens," Pioneer Essay Collection, California Room, San Jose Public Library, 1978.

_____."Naglee's Brandy Image . . . ," *Wine Spectator*, 2/16/1981.

_____."A Viticultural Mystery Solved: The Historical Origins of Zinfandel in California," *California History*, (Summer, 1978), 114-129.

_____."Wine Flummery," *New West*, (September 24, 1979), 45-50. The misuse of history by some modern wineries.

Thompson & West. *Historical Atlas Map of Santa Clara County*, San Francisco, 1876.

Thompson, Bob. *California Wine*, Menlo Park, 1973.

_____.*Guide to California's Wine Country*, Menlo Park, 1968 and 1979.

Waite, Frona Eunice. *Wines & Vines of California*, San Francisco, 1889.

Wickson, E.J. *California Nurserymen and the Plant Industry, 1850-1910*, Los Angeles, 1921.

INDEX

188

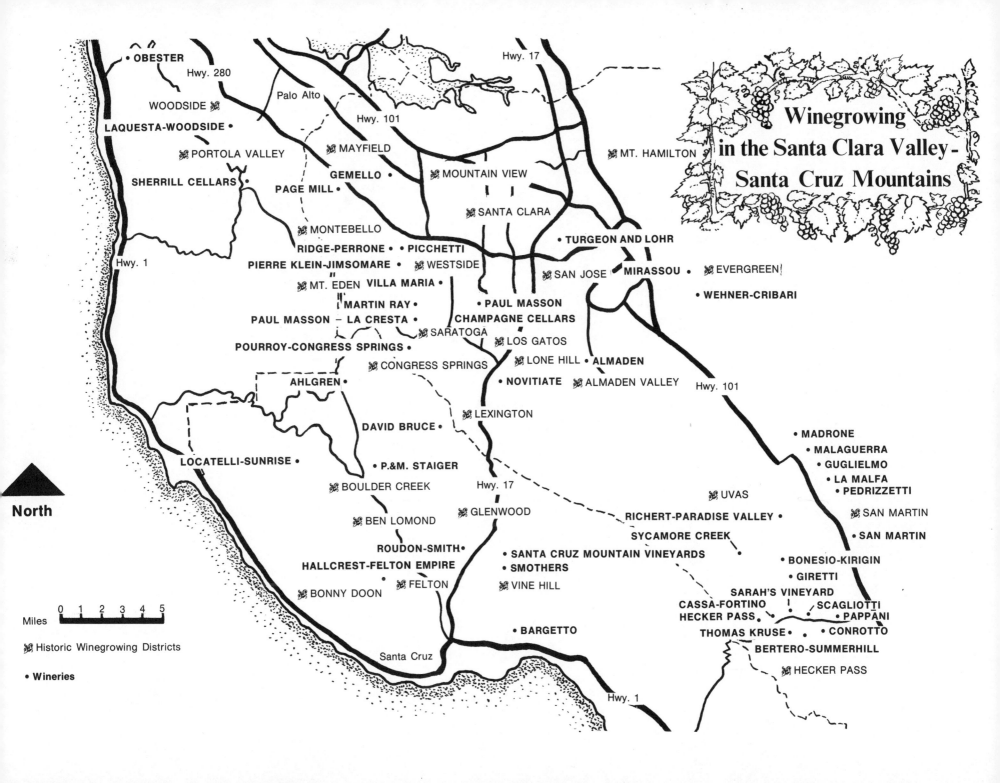

Winegrowing in the Santa Clara Valley - Santa Cruz Mountains

• OBESTER
Hwy. 280

WOODSIDE 🥀

LAQUESTA-WOODSIDE •

Palo Alto

Hwy. 101

🥀 MAYFIELD

🥀 PORTOLA VALLEY

Hwy. 17

🥀 MT. HAMILTON 🥀

SHERRILL CELLARS •

GEMELLO •

🥀 MOUNTAIN VIEW

PAGE MILL •

🥀 SANTA CLARA

Hwy. 1

🥀 MONTEBELLO

• TURGEON AND LOHR

RIDGE-PERRONE • PICCHETTI

PIERRE KLEIN-JIMSOMARE • 🥀 WESTSIDE

🥀 SAN JOSE MIRASSOU • 🥀 EVERGREEN!

🥀 MT. EDEN VILLA MARIA •

• WEHNER-CRIBARI

• MARTIN RAY •

• PAUL MASSON

PAUL MASSON – LA CRESTA •

CHAMPAGNE CELLARS

🥀 SARATOGA

POURROY-CONGRESS SPRINGS •

🥀 LOS GATOS

🥀 CONGRESS SPRINGS

• LONE HILL • ALMADEN

AHLGREN •

• NOVITIATE 🥀 ALMADEN VALLEY

Hwy. 101

🥀 LEXINGTON

• MADRONE

DAVID BRUCE •

• MALAGUERRA

• GUGLIELMO

LOCATELLI-SUNRISE •

• P.&M. STAIGER

• LA MALFA

• PEDRIZZETTI

🥀 BOULDER CREEK

Hwy. 17

🥀 UVAS

🥀 BEN LOMOND

🥀 GLENWOOD

RICHERT-PARADISE VALLEY •

🥀 SAN MARTIN

SYCAMORE CREEK

• SAN MARTIN

ROUDON-SMITH•

• SANTA CRUZ MOUNTAIN VINEYARDS

• BONESIO-KIRIGIN

HALLCREST-FELTON EMPIRE

• SMOTHERS

• GIRETTI

🥀 FELTON

🥀 VINE HILL

SARAH'S VINEYARD

🥀 BONNY DOON

CASSA-FORTINO

• SCAGLIOTTI

HECKER PASS

• PAPPANI

• BARGETTO

THOMAS KRUSE •

• CONROTTO

BERTERO-SUMMERHILL

Santa Cruz

🥀 HECKER PASS

North

0 1 2 3 4 5

Miles

🥀 Historic Winegrowing Districts

• Wineries

Hwy. 1